TESTIMONIALS

Ken MacHarg (Latin America, Europe, Central Asia)

To me, serving an international church is a blessing and a joy. I no longer have a strong desire or sense of call to serve a church in the U.S. As a third-culture person and a global nomad, I can very easily fall into conversation with an expat—much more than with someone in our small town back home. I find the people fascinating, the churches exciting, the ministry fulfilling.

John Carlock

We have been in Cairo for going on five years. HCC was our home church before I began pastoring two years ago. This was a new experience for us having come from another field where we did not have the option of an international church. We were part of an Arabic congregation. It was very difficult for the family, especially for the kids who did not have Bible education or youth group in English. So coming to Cairo and having an international church was a real blessing. Many of our members are involved in ministry in the church community. There are families in the church whose kids all go to the same private school here in this area. Our kids were able to be part of an English speaking youth group. Most of the other kids were missionary kids and knew what it was like to be living overseas with parents in ministry. And there is children's ministry as well. So we found the international church was very beneficial for our family. It brought a lot of healing to myself and a lot of spiritual strength to our family. Our boys did very well with the youth group, built strong relationships, and got involved playing guitar and leading in worship. They were challenged in their prayer life and through youth retreats and even a mission trip to Kenya where they got involved in urban ministry in Nairobi. All of this was through an international church here in Cairo. We can certainly see the benefit of it and the opportunity it has to the not only to the expatriate community. Although we don't intentionally do outreach out to nationals, we do have nationals who come in. We have nationals who are married to expats. Some get involved and build relationships. It is an avenue where they feel comfortable. And they feel welcome whereas in the indigenous church they may not feel welcome. So the international church can provide a number of benefits to the expatriate community as well as nationals.

David Fisher (Lisbon, Madrid)

I find international church to be particularly satisfying for a few reasons. First that it is there at all and available for expats and students abroad to have a source of Christian community and teaching and support. It is powerful for that reason alone. Beyond that I appreciate the freedom that many of the churches have to focus on the core of the faith and not get bogged down in differences or distinctives of practice that separate denominational churches from each other and so fragment the greater Church. Often times as well, international churches offer and even encourage people to get involved and give them volunteer ministry opportunities that they can take advantage of and learn from and bless others through.

Barry Gaeddert (London)

I loved the privilege to meet people from all over the world. It was a humbling experience to discover the rich variety of places where people had lived, whether they were born there or had spent time living and working there. I also appreciated the challenge to help order the church's priorities. There is no time or space for arguing over denominational differences and issues that, ultimately, do not matter. In an international church you learn to discern what really is important (the Gospel!) and focus your ministries on that in a way that invites, encourages, and supports people from a wide variety of backgrounds on their journeys with it.

Steve McMichael (Tangier, Zambia)

Working in international church ministry allows one to glimpse the diversity of the body of Christ across ethnic, cultural, and economic lines. It expands one's appreciation and awe for the grace of God globally. It also allows one to contribute to an ever-changing community of believers that touches all parts of a city, and many parts of the world.

Louwrens Scheepers (Fes)

The seven years in Morocco as the pastor of the International Church in Fes were some of the best years for us as a family. It was the best years for me in ministry! I learned so much about myself, about being a truly diverse family of God. I learned about being church in new ways and every Sunday was an amazing experience worshiping God together as people from so many different languages and cultures.

If I had this guide in my hands before coming to Morocco, it would have made our transition into Morocco so much easier. This is not only a guide for pastors, it will also be helpful to those who know they are going to a foreign country and want to join an international church. All the practical illustrations from pastors in different contexts help to make this guide a very helpful tool for any one involved in an international church.

John Mullen (Prague)

Nineteen years ago I jumped blindly into international church ministry. How fortunate are those who have the opportunity to read this guide before they jump. Most international pastors do not last long on the field. Ironically, stable pastoral leadership is more needed in an international church context where lay leaders are rotating through. I believe this guide will go a long way to give leaders the footing and grounding needed to serve long-term in an international church ministry.

David Pederson (Athens, Seoul)

Jack Wald lends his extensive pastoral experience to build upon the growing body of work that helps to explain, encourage, and expand the phenomenon of the English-speaking expatriate churches worldwide. The need for serious study and application of biblical principles to the international church leadership is growing as people relocate, retire, do business, and seek refuge in places far from home. As the evangelical world catches wind of diaspora ministry, the need for practical direction for pastors will grow as well. And Jack has done a thorough job of filling the void for the hands-on leader of the church of the global nomads: the expatriate community of followers of Christ. This handbook is a necessary guide for the expatriate Christian and for church leaders worldwide.

A GUIDE TO INTERNATIONAL CHURCH MINISTRY:

PASTORING A PARADE

JACK WALD

To the members of Rabat International Church.
Over the past fifteen years you have come and gone,
but you remain in my heart.

The first church to ever exist was not a small country church comprised of people of the same cultural heritage, rather it was an international fellowship of several thousand strong gathered in a major city.

—David Packer, *Look Who God Let into the Church*

CONTENTS

PREFACE

My Call to Ministry at Rabat International Church

When I travel in the U.S., I am often asked what brought me to Morocco. To many people who meet me, it seems as exotic as it did to me when I first considered a call to be pastor of Rabat International Church (RIC). I had lived for one year in Hamburg, Germany, after high school. I took business trips to Mexico. I spoke at conferences in South America. I had business trips to Europe and Japan. I traveled with my family to Europe and had a wonderful safari experience in Tanzania. I was not unaware of the world but had no idea I would one day be working overseas.

I first surrendered to Jesus when I was in my second year of university in Boston. I was fortunate to be a part of the Seekers ministry (college and graduate age group) at Park Street Church and it was there that I gained a solid foundation for my faith.

I planned to apply to medical school, but then in the most clear way God has ever spoken to me, I knew I should go to seminary. I resisted this call for three months as I bargained increasing percentages of my potential salary and months per year as a missionary doctor, but I finally surrendered and applied to seminary. After graduating from Gordon-Conwell Theological Seminary, I worked at odd jobs for a year while my wife finished her university studies, and then I began serving as a youth minister in a Methodist church in West Virginia. After one year as a youth pastor, I began serving as pastor of two, small Presbyterian churches in eastern Ohio and was ordained into the PCUSA in May 1981.[1]

---

[1] The churches were then part of the United Presbyterian Church in the United States of America, which merged with the Presbyterian Church in the United States in 1983 to form the Presbyterian Church (USA).

After six and a half years of ministry, I was burned out and went to work with Richard Lovelace, church history professor at Gordon-Conwell Theological Seminary. He was creating a new organization to work with renewal elements of the mainline denominations, but after six months he had health problems and that path came to an end.

From there I went to work with my father in a family business. I spent thirteen years in the business world, selling ultraviolet curable printing inks to label makers. In February 1999, this business was sold, and I was unsure what I would do next. That April our church in Princeton, New Jersey, had a missions conference and a couple, Abe and Joyce Wiebe, who were working with Arab World Ministries, stayed with us. As we talked, Abe told me a church in Rabat, Morocco, was looking for a pastor, and he thought I would be a good fit.

I don't remember exactly what I said, but it could be summarized as, "Whatever," because it seemed too remote a possibility for me to take seriously. But I exchanged emails with the church (which was then called Rabat Protestant Fellowship—RPF) and I was invited to come for an interview in September 1999. For two weeks I preached and met many of the people in the church. A short time later, they invited me to be pastor of RIC and I arrived in January 2000.

I love Rabat International Church. I like to say that churches around the world pick their best members and send them to Morocco so I have the privilege of preaching to an all-star congregation. I have been encouraged by the members of RIC. I have been taught by the members of RIC. I am a very different follower of Jesus than I was before I came fifteen years ago, and, to a large extent, it is the people of this church over the years who have enriched my life.

WHAT INSPIRED ME TO WRITE
THIS GUIDE

It is the positive experience of my years at RIC that inspired me to write *A Guide to International Church Ministry*. I began Doctor of Ministry studies at Gordon-Conwell Theological Seminary in 2010 so I could explore in more detail what had made my experience at RIC so wonderful. After I completed my DMin and graduated in May 2015, I decided to make the guide I wrote available so others could benefit from it.

I share my opinions but I am under no illusion that anyone will agree with everything that I say. As much as possible, I have tried to include points of view from other international pastors so that this guide will be helpful to a broader range of leaders. What I write is not meant to be a rule book or how-to book for international church ministry. It is meant to help those already working in international churches, as well as those interested in international church ministry, to be better prepared to lead as they think through their own perspective of church life issues.

In this guide I discuss international church distinctives and apply them to the life and ministry of an international church. As I received feedback from international pastors and church leaders, I incorporated their comments to provide a wider range of perspectives on these issues.

In the range of international churches, RIC is on one end of the spectrum. There are cities with multiple international churches; Rabat has just one English-speaking international church. There are cities where the international churches have a significant number of national believers who attend; RIC rarely has Moroccans who attend. There are international churches with a significant part of the congregation who live permanently in the city where the church is located; RIC is highly transitional. There are international churches in countries that are sympathetic to Christian faith; RIC exists in a country that is 99 percent Muslim.

I discovered that despite the differences among international churches, there is a large part of what each international church experiences that is shared in common. There may still have to be a bit of translating of the experience of RIC to another international church, but there will be a lot of resonance.

My hope is that those who read this guide will be encouraged to use their spiritual gifts in one of the international churches of the world and be better prepared for life and ministry as they serve in an international church.

INTERNATIONAL CHURCH LEADERS WHO READ AND COMMENTED ON THE GUIDE

I was pleased to have twenty-three international church pastors and leaders who read and commented on the guide. They helped me expand the guide into topics I had overlooked and added a broader perspective. You will see some of their comments as you read through the guide.

(Name followed by where they served in leadership)

Greg Anderson: London; Hong Kong

Sue Beaman: Rabat; Jordan; Cyprus

John Carlock: Cairo

Ray Cobb: Fes

John Findley: Fes

Daphne Fisher: Lisbon; Madrid

David Fisher: Lisbon; Madrid

Barry Gaeddert: London

Wendy Haugtvedt: Dubai

Patrick Havens: Rabat

Roger Hesch: Rabat

Connie Huffer: Rabat; Jordan; Cyprus

Elliot Lamptey: Rabat

Deon Malan: Marrakech

Chris Martin: Casablanca

Steve McDaniel: Rabat

Ken MacHarg: Panama; Ecuador; Costa Rica; Honduras; Prague; Kyrgyzstan

Steve McMichael: Tangier; Zambia

John Mullen: Prague

David Packer: Singapore; Stuttgart

David Pederson: Athens; Seoul

Louwrens Scheepers: Fes

A U.S. pastor exploring overseas ministry but has not told his congregation he is thinking about a change.

CHAPTER ONE

WHAT IS AN INTERNATIONAL CHURCH?

It is helpful to remember that the birth of the church, recorded in the book of Acts, took place in an international context. As David Packer points out, "... the first church to ever exist was not a small country church comprised of people of the same cultural heritage, rather it was an international fellowship of several thousand strong gathered in a major city."[2]

The outpouring of the Holy Spirit did not come to the disciples of Jesus in Galilee. It took place in Jerusalem but not when Jerusalem was largely composed of Hebrew-speaking Jews. It took place during the Feast of Weeks, the harvest festival, second of the three annual festivals in Jerusalem.

As a consequence, Jerusalem was filled with Jewish visitors from around the Roman world. Fifteen people groups are listed in Acts 2 as having been present at Pentecost.[3] The outpouring of the Holy Spirit at Pentecost was the birth of the church and the church was revealed to be universal, for all people.

This is God's work, bringing all the diverse people of the world into his church. The church of Jesus is an international body with people from every nation, tribe, people, and language.[4] If we are created to live for eternity with Jesus in heaven, then international churches will help us prepare for our home

---

[2] David Packer, *Look Who God Let into the Church* (n.p.: Growth Points International, 2013), 9.

[3] Acts 2:9–11: "Parthians, Medes and Elamites; residents of Mesopotamia, Judea and Cappadocia, Pontus and Asia, Phrygia and Pamphylia, Egypt and the parts of Libya near Cyrene; visitors from Rome (both Jews and converts to Judaism); Cretans and Arabs—we hear them declaring the wonders of God in our own tongues!'"

[4] Revelation 7:9.

in a way the homogenous church communities that dominate Christian faith cannot.

What do we mean when we talk about international churches? It is not as easy as saying that an international church is one that represents many nations around the world. For example, if a church in Tennessee has a Japanese citizen who joins the church, that does not make it an international church. When international students at a university in the U.S. attend a local church, that does not make the church an international church.

Missional International Church Network (MICN) is, as its name suggests, a network of international churches that are mostly based in Asia. This is how they define international churches: "International churches (ICs) are those churches around the world that primarily serve people of various nationalities (expatriates) and church backgrounds living outside their passport (home) countries."[5]

My focus in this guide will be on English-speaking international churches. English may be a second, third, or fourth language for many of those who attend, but English will be the common language in the church.

International churches are made up of people who, for the most part, are passing through. There may be spouses of nationals who attend and whose long-term life is in the country of their spouse, but those are the exceptions. In closed countries where there are restrictions on national followers of Jesus, there is a distinction between the house churches where local followers of Jesus attend and the churches attended by foreigners. Although some international churches meet in homes, most meet in more traditional church buildings or houses rented or owned by the church community. The most clear distinction between local churches and international churches is that those who attend the local churches will most likely live their senior years in their country, while that is unlikely for those who attend the international churches. As a consequence, in my fifteen years as pastor of RIC, we have had only seven funerals for members of our church.

For several reasons, it is difficult to say how many international churches exist in the world. First, there are many informal small groups that meet in homes. Second, in countries where churches have to meet secretly, believers do not publicize their existence. Third, there are many new international churches being created but there is no single network that tracks these churches and the various organizations that try to track international churches do not have

⁵ "What Is an IC?" *Missional International Church Network (MICN)*, http://micn.org/?page_
id=239.

complete lists. When I looked at five networks of international churches,[6] RIC was not included on any of the lists.

Ken MacHarg,[7] who has written articles about international churches in recent decades and who has served as pastor in eight international churches in Latin America, Europe, and Asia, has estimated there are more than 1,200 international churches around the world. About one-third of those are denominational (mostly Baptist, Presbyterian, Lutheran, or Anglican). The rest of the churches are intentionally interdenominational.[8]

David Pederson, an international pastor who has written about international church ministry, commented: "Based on the small communities reported from Japan, Saudi Arabia, China, and observed in Korea and Athens, I estimate that these communities more than double the known expatriate English-speaking churches which stands currently at about 1,200 congregations/chaplaincies."[9]

Among all these international churches, some features will be more predominant and others less so, giving each international church its character. An international church may be located in a city where there are multiple international churches; others are the only international church in the city. Some international churches have a significant number of national believers who attend; others rarely have local believers in their services. There are international churches with a significant percentage of long-term members; others are highly transitional. There are international churches in countries that are sympathetic or at least benign to the Christian faith; others exist in dominant Muslim, Buddhist, or Hindu populations. Some international churches have a high percentage of missionaries, students, or businessmen and businesswomen; others have a broader mix of those who attend.

A BRIEF HISTORY OF INTERNATIONAL CHURCHES

If you go to international church websites, you can often find histories of those particular churches, but with the scarcity of literature focused on

---

[6] International Churches Network, http://internationalchurches.net/; Fellowship of European International Churches, http://feic.org/; The Network of International Churches, http://www.internationalcongregations.net/; Association of International Churches in Europe and the Middle East, http://aiceme.net/; Churches Abroad, http://www.churchesabroad.com/.

[7] For a list of Ken MacHarg's many articles, see http://www.missionaryjournalist.net/ and https://kensintrospect.wordpress.com/.

[8] Ken MacHarg, "An Unusual Breed," Missionary Journalist, http://www.missionaryjournalist.net/images/Intl_Congregations-_An_Unusual_Breed.pdf.

[9] Pederson, *Expatriate Ministry*, 78.

international churches, it is difficult to find a comprehensive history of them. Ken MacHarg provided this brief history:

> Some international churches were started way back in the 1800s by missionaries and in the early 1900s. They were all called Union Churches because they were genuinely a coming together of people from various Protestant denominations to form one church that represented and served all of those bodies. There are numerous international churches still operating that carry the name Union Church including in London, Frankfurt, Mexico City, Guatemala City, Bogota, Panama City, Manila, Tokyo (and several other cities in Japan), a few in Korea, etc. Even the many international churches that were started after World War II up until the 1980s or so were intentionally developed as being multidenominational.
>
> In more recent times, however, there has been a movement to start new international churches by groups that are tied or semi-related to some denominational movements such as Vineyard, Calvary Chapel, and others. While they have indicated that they welcome people from multiple denominations (and they genuinely do) they also take on strong characteristics of those founding bodies. These churches are primarily found in Europe and retirement spots in Latin America such as Costa Rica.

A BRIEF HISTORY OF
RABAT INTERNATIONAL CHURCH

Since this guide draws from my experience at RIC, it is helpful to know a bit of RIC's history. The history of an international church is often quite vague because of its high rate of transition. David Pederson comments that, "The high-turnover church needs a sense of history. If you remain in a high-turnover church for more than three years, you are the resident historian."[10] So while I am the current resident historian of RIC, I am fortunate to have a more complete history of RIC from the pastor who preceded me, Roger Hesch:

> It is my understanding that the current Rabat International Church began in the early 1950s as a bible study group at the U.S. embassy in Rabat. It continued as an on again and off again study, changing as embassy personnel changed, until the early 1960s.
>
> During the 1960s more of a formal church body began to form with meetings taking place on Sundays and worship times being added

---

[10] Pederson, *Expatriate Ministry*, 100.

to the more informal Bible studies. I do not know exactly, but I seem to remember that there were several one year or more periods during that decade when pastors served the gathering, either because they were bi-vocational leaders assigned to the embassy or had come into the country for other reasons and became associated with the group of fellow Christians living in the city. I believe that it was at some point late in the 1960s that an agreement was made with the French Protestant church to begin meeting in their building in town rather than just in homes.

In the 1970s, I believe, because the meeting was now at a church building, several more non-embassy expatriates began attending. Most were either married to Moroccans or business people who were located in Rabat. They began to make up a more steady congregation that was both non-American and not rotating in and out every two to three years. Sometime late in the 1970s I think the Southern Baptists from the USA began to allow one of their overseas personnel to serve the congregation on a regular basis as a pastor, thus providing for them a legal "Christian" presence in the country. SB's also began to supply pastors to other small congregations in Fes and Tangier during these days and the early 1980s.

During the 1980s Rabat Protestant Fellowship—or RPF—was meeting each week at the building owned by the French Evangelicals and paying most of the bills to keep the building open. The French Protestant congregation was fewer than ten people at many points. RPF began to reach out to a wider segment of the expatriate community and pastors from the SB stayed more years giving the church continuity.

By the time I was asked to join RPF in 1995, the Baptist identity of the church was firmly entrenched and being resented by many who were from non-Baptist backgrounds. There were several Christian groups represented in Rabat who were talking about dividing out into smaller meetings which would more readily reflect non-Baptist backgrounds. Once a month the Anglican church was having a communion service for those desiring a more liturgical worship time. Some were wanting a more Pentecostal service. Some were wanting a "church" and not a fellowship (RPF). Some wanted a larger Christian presence in the country.

During my days at RPF we changed the name from Rabat Protestant Fellowship to simply RPF and then once people forgot what RPF stood for we began saying RPF International Church to clarify. We began to include in our Sunday morning service practices and elements from a wider variety of denominational backgrounds and cultural backgrounds that helped to draw the greater English-speaking Christian community in Rabat together. We helped a Korean congregation launch and worked with the French-speaking congregation to hold joint services, knitting the Christian community together in more formal ways. We began the formation of an association of Protestant churches in Morocco and assisted in the formation of new churches in Marrakesh and Casablanca modeled after the congregation in Rabat.

Toward the end of Roger Hesch's pastorate in Rabat, the Southern Baptists made a decision to no longer supply international churches with pastors, so when I arrived in Rabat in January, 2000, I (ordained in the PCUSA) was the first non-Baptist pastor in many years.

MAKEUP OF THE RIC COMMUNITY

The community of RIC is very broad. A large number of those who attend are university students from sub-Saharan Africa and the islands of the Atlantic and Pacific who come to study in Morocco. These students are sponsored by a UNESCO program that pays for their tuition and offers a small scholarship for expenses. The students who come from English-speaking countries spend a year in Rabat studying French. When they pass their French exam, they are then assigned to universities around the country, including Rabat, for their formal university education. This means RIC has a new group of students every year, only a small part of whom will stay in Rabat for the next four or five years. RIC also has a smaller number of American students who come to Rabat to study Arabic for a semester. Most are in university, but some high-school students have come as well. These young men and women are here for a semester or two before they return to their high school or university.

Because Rabat is the capital city of Morocco, RIC has diplomats and military attachés who attend the church. These people generally stay for two to four years before they are reassigned to other posts. There are also teachers of English as a second language and teachers in the American School or one of the other schools in Rabat. RIC has men and women in business who are assigned to Morocco for a period of time and a few who are trying to start businesses. Academics (Fulbright Scholars and others) come to do research in

Morocco. There are also Peace Corps volunteers (U.S.) and KOICA volunteers (the Korean equivalent).

Other parts of the RIC community include people from India and the Philippines who have come to work for upper-class Moroccans. There are also illegal migrants who have left their home country (mostly sub-Saharan Africans) and are trying to raise funds to pay the smugglers to cross into Spain. In addition, there are a number of women married to Moroccans who have made Morocco their home.

Over the years I have been pastor, RIC has averaged between 150-200 people who attend the weekly service. Although RIC meets in the capital city of a Muslim country, the weekend is still Saturday and Sunday because of the French who colonized Morocco in the early 1900s.

WHAT IS LIFE LIKE IN AN INTERNATIONAL CHURCH?

When you consider all the cities of the world where international churches are found, it is easy to see that on the surface, churches will not be homogenous. But if you look below the surface, these churches have many similarities that make someone from one international church resonate with the experience of someone at another international church. One picture of what life is like in an international church comes from an article written by Ken MacHarg:

> They're called expatriates—expats for short. An unusual breed of people, they live outside of their home country, working, studying, serving, running, seeking. Several million U.S. citizens call Mexico, South Africa, Thailand, France and a host of other foreign locations home. Most of them are conventional expats. They are people who go abroad with a definite purpose for a defined length of time. They are diplomats sent by their governments, business executives deployed by international companies, students and professors pursuing educational goals, engineers and technical people working for oil companies or other organizations, relief and development experts seeking to improve the world and missionaries sent to serve the Lord. . . . Those who have lived outside of their native land form a unique culture with worldwide ties. They are known as Third-Culture people. In one sense they belong nowhere and in another sense they belong everywhere. Living in another culture, they never really become a part of their adopted land, even if they marry someone from their new home.

They are always foreigners to some extent, set apart by language, cultural and political backgrounds and styles of life. However, having lived outside of their native land, they view the world differently and find it very difficult to return home and fit into the isolationist patterns they discover that they left behind. They understand international air fares, visa regulations and international issues that no one at home knows or cares about. They have seen political coups, eaten exotic foods, traveled to remote beaches and mountains and experienced events not even imagined by their former neighbors and friends. This culture has its own set of struggles, questions, successes and failures. They are often lonely in the midst of a big city, lost in another culture, cut-off from the familiar with a longing to return yet a resistance to going back home.[11]

People in an international church never tire of talking about the remarkable diversity of the church. One week, in a Sunday School class of eighteen people at RIC, there were twelve nationalities represented. A recent church board had seven people with six nations represented: Columbia, Germany, South Korea, Ghana, India, and the U.S. A year before, the board included people from Britain, the U.S., Ghana, Swaziland, and Germany.

David Packer (Singapore, Stuttgart) comments on why people come to an international church:

- they had previously gone overseas for studies or work and are now back in their home culture but not entirely comfortable with their own national church

- they are thinking about making a move abroad and the international church gives them an opportunity to meet new people of different cultures, practice honing their language skills, and help them network into the new culture which they are moving toward. So they have either gone abroad, are not living abroad, or plan to go abroad.[12]

---

[11] Ken MacHarg, "An Unusual Breed."

[12] Packer, *Look Who God Let into the Church*, 40–41.

CHAPTER TWO

WHAT IS THE DIFFERENCE BETWEEN AN INTERNATIONAL CHURCH AND A NATIONAL CHURCH?

FEWER OPTIONS

For English-speakers in most international cities, answering the question, "Where should we go to church?" is simpler than in their home country. I once ate at a restaurant in Savannah, Georgia, that listed on the placemat the names of all the churches in town. Savannah has a population of 136,565 and has 264 churches (122 Baptist, 22 Methodist, 20 non-denominational, 12 Church of Christ, 10 Church of God, 10 Episcopalian, 10 Christian, 7 Presbyterian, 7 Lutheran, 6 Catholic, 6 Holiness, 4 Assembly of God, and 28 others). When someone moves to Savannah they go church shopping and find the church that most suits them. When they find the church that most suits them, it is likely they will find a church with a lot of people like themselves, with similar interests and backgrounds.

But when the same person moves to a foreign city, they will not find many options. In cities like Paris and Rome, there are three or four English-speaking international churches. In Chiang Mai, Thailand, a hub for Christian organizations working in Southeast Asia, there are at least six English-speaking, Protestant international churches.[13] In Rabat, there is one English-speaking

---

[13]   The Gathering (Southern Baptist), Chiang Mai Christian Fellowship (nondenominational, conservative evangelical), Chiang Mai Community Church (founded in the late 1800s), House of Praise International (Pentecostal Australian), Vineyard Church, All-Saints Chiang Mai Church (Anglican/Episcopalian).

Protestant church. The Catholic church has an English Mass, sometimes each week and sometimes once a month, depending on the priests who are available.

DIVERSITY

The lack of options leads to diversity in international churches. In a community with many church options, the natural tendency for people is to coalesce around common backgrounds and understandings. But in an international church, by necessity, people come from many different backgrounds.

International churches are diverse nationally. RIC currently has approximately forty nationalities and over the years has had members from more than seventy countries.

The diversity of an international church is not limited to the countries people come from; it also comes from the number of countries where people have lived. At a recent dinner, we had couples from India, South Korea, Britain, Armenia, Colombia, Palestine, and the U.S. (one couple was was British/Armenian and another was Palestinian/American). We went around the room listing the countries we had lived in for at least one year and people mentioned five to ten countries each. With only three countries between us, my wife and I were in the minority.

This leads to rich and interesting conversations. Last year, two young men on a motorbike deliberately hit my car in order to cause an accident and gain access to the contents of the car. The scam is that while I get out to see if they are hurt, one of them argues with me about who was at fault. Meanwhile the other gets into the car, takes whatever can be found, and then the two of them run off. When I told people in the church what happened, they shared their experiences with this and similar scams they had experienced in Liberia, Tanzania, and other countries where they have lived. At another meal, a group of us began to discuss the relative safety of working in Iraq and Afghanistan, all from personal experience. People in an international church not only come from all over the world, but they have also been all over the world. We live in the united nations.

International churches are diverse racially. On an average Sunday RIC has 200 people, representing every race. RIC is composed of about 50 percent sub-Saharan Africans, 10 percent Asians, and 40 percent Europeans/North and South Americans. Every continent, except Antarctica, is well represented.

With people from so many nations, there are also many cultures represented in an international church and each culture brings a distinct perspective. People have different world views from which they approach the Bible and Christian living. They view and treat the pastor differently. They view death differently. They have different expectations about how we fellowship, how the church building should be used, etc.

International churches are diverse theologically and denominationally. RIC has over forty denominations represented on an average Sunday. There are dispensationalists and Pentecostals sitting side-by-side. There are high church and low church representatives. There are people from Quaker, Mennonite, and Brethren backgrounds as well as those from mainline denominations and small Pentecostal churches. There are some from a Catholic background. People come from both meditative and exuberant styles of worship. An international church reflects the denominations and worship styles of the world.

International churches are diverse economically as well. Because there are limited church options, the poor and the rich come to the same church. At RIC, there are people who receive a good salary as diplomats and can spend as much for lunch as others in the church will spend for food for a week or more. Some drive to church, and others walk because they cannot afford the four dirhams (about fifty cents USD) it costs to ride the bus. There are migrants who beg on the streets during the week to try to raise funds to make the crossing into Spain, and others who fly to their home country once or twice a year.

There are people who sleep on mattresses, five or six in a one-room apartment and others who live in grand villas. I live in a less grand villa, and at a church potluck held in our home, one of the migrants came up to me and asked, "Who else lives here with you and your wife?" He could not comprehend how two people could live in a villa with so much space.

International churches are diverse educationally. At RIC, we have those with doctorates as well as those who never completed high school. RIC has students studying in the local university as well as those who have been educated on the streets.

International churches are diverse linguistically. It is unusual to find someone who does not speak a second language and not at all unusual to find someone who speaks four or five languages. We were all impressed when a man from Switzerland visited RIC a few years ago and was able to speak fifteen languages.

One area where international churches are not so diverse is age. People tend to retire to their home countries so there are not many people over the age of sixty. Most of the members of RIC are in their twenties or thirties.

TRANSITIONAL

A third distinctive of international churches is that they are more transitional than most churches. Pastoring an international church in Morocco has been described as pastoring a parade.[14] You extend your hand to welcome someone and soon you are slowly lifting it up to wave goodbye to them. When RIC has a farewell potluck meal for someone, there are usually people at the potluck who just came to church for the first time that Sunday or perhaps the week before. At RIC, 60 percent of the congregation changes every two years.[15]

An illustration of the transitional nature of the church is a couple who lived in Rabat for twenty-three years. Over those years, their home was a center for fellowship and meetings for RIC. If ever RIC had pillars of the church, they were pillars. When they finally left for the U.S., it was a big loss. But three years later when they returned for a visit, only a small part of the church knew who they were. If I were to step down as pastor and leave, and then return in three years for a visit, the same would be true for me.

MINORITY FAITH

A further distinctive of RIC is that it meets in a country that is 99 percent Muslim. Christians are a tiny minority. This is also the case for international churches located in dominant Hindu and Buddhist countries.

In the rest of the guide, I will show how these distinctives of an international church: limited or no other options, highly diverse, highly transitional, and existing as a minority faith affect the life and ministry of an international church.

---

[14] This was told to me by Darrell Pack who was pastor of the Casablanca International Church during my first years in Morocco.

[15] This is an approximate statistic. Currently, 40.5 percent of our 200 average attendance on Sunday morning are members of the church. Of these, 60.5 percent became members in 2011 to 2014. There is a more stable core in the church. 18.5 percent of the members have been members for over ten years. 60 percent of those who attend weekly services are not members and are more transitional than the members of the church.

CHAPTER THREE

HOW INTERNATIONAL CHURCH DISTINCTIVES AFFECT CHURCH LIFE

PREACHING

Preaching to a multidenominational, multicultural, multinational congregation presents interesting challenges. One of the most obvious is the use
of illustrations.

ILLUSTRATIONS

When I was preaching through the book of Romans and wanted an
illustration for the struggle of our two natures in Romans 7, I thought of Robert
Louis Stevenson's story, *The Strange Case of Dr. Jekyll and Mr. Hyde*. The problem
is that his story, and much of Western literature, is unknown to a majority of
our congregation. I had a similar problem when I wanted to illustrate Paul's
understanding of the doctrine of sanctification with the relationship between
Don Quixote and his Dulcinea. In both cases I had to take time to explain the
story before I could make the point. I had to assume people knew nothing about
these stories.

This is true of literature, movies, music, and it is also true of sports. The
world plays football, but not the football Americans know. The world plays
what Americans call soccer and when I use this sport as an analogy, I need to
be careful to call it football.

The World Cup means much more to people in our church than the World
Series. (How can it be the "World Series" when the teams who compete all play

in North America?) The world does not play baseball and the game is a mystery to most people in our congregation.

I have heard from more than one member of an international church that the American pastor had a fondness for American football or baseball illustrations, despite the fact that the congregation did not understand these sports and did not get the point being made.

It is not simply a matter of using sports as an analogy; the problem is that there are so many expressions used in common American English that come from sports. Take baseball for instance. "He hit it out of the park." "Give me a ballpark figure." "She's batting a thousand." "You've got to cover your bases." "He threw me a curve ball." "They're playing hardball." "That came out of left field." "You have to step up to the plate." People not familiar with baseball will not understand what these idioms mean.

One of the expressions I like to use in talking about someone from the First World who is successful is, "He thinks he hit a home run but forgets that he was born on third base." This is a great line but if I use it, I have to consider if the line is good enough to justify taking the time to explain the game of baseball so people can understand what it means.

I once wanted to use the game of hide-and-seek where the one seeking calls out at the end, "Olly olly oxen free." but had to consider how well known that child's game is outside of the U.S. and maybe England. I used this as an illustration but had to explain the game.

I have learned to speak about kilometers rather than miles and kilograms rather than pounds, and most times I reference both measures and weights so that everyone will understand.

Steve McMichael (Tangier, Zambia) gave an illustration from his experience in Zambia:

> While teaching a Bible school class about culture and hermeneutics, I learned something about culture myself. I wanted to illustrate how culture is always changing and was applying it to apparel. To this end I was explaining how, when back in the States, I had attended a church with over 2,000 in attendance and the pastor came out to speak wearing only an open collared shirt and pants.
>
> My point was he wasn't wearing a suit and tie. But "pants" in the British English that Zambians speak, means underwear. So my emphasis that he had on ONLY an open-collared shirt and PANTS left them

giggling like middle school children and my point was completely lost, but the lesson was learned. Culture is continuously adjusting.

BROADEN CULTURAL REFERENCES

In preparing a sermon, my instinct is to go to the cultural references I know best, but that takes me to the U.S., and in a congregation that is less than 15 percent American I need to learn about other cultures and use people from those cultures as illustrations. For example, I once used a story told by Bishop Festo Kivengere about three men who were publically killed by Idi Amin in Uganda. They died joyfully, with faith in Jesus. It is a powerful story and a much better example for the half of the congregation that is sub-Saharan African than a story of a U.S. missionary who died for Jesus.

When I was talking about the danger of being on a river that will soon take you over a waterfall, my first instinct was to talk about the Niagara River and Niagara Falls. But instead I talked about the Zambezi River and Victoria Falls. I use the geography and animals of the world, not simply the geography and animals of North America.

For a period of time, I met each week on Tuesday morning to talk about the upcoming sermon with four other people, two Western women and one Western man, all of whom had spent many years in the Middle East and North Africa, and a sub-Saharan African. I got valuable insights about the text and how it is viewed by different cultures and I got valuable illustrations that spoke more broadly to the whole congregation. With the transitional nature of international churches, this meeting did not take place for more than a year, but now has resumed—much to my delight. I keep my ears open when talking with people from the congregation through the week and sometimes ask how they would illustrate, from their cultural perspective, a point in the sermon.

WORD CHOICES

For many people in our congregation, English is a second or third or fourth language. Even for those who speak English as a first language, their level of education may not give them the same vocabulary that I have at my disposal. This means that I have to be conscious about what words I use. Because I like words, I have a difficult time throwing away the perfect word to use in a sentence. But when I am aware that not all people will understand that word, I add a phrase that translates the meaning of the word as well.

"An Aussie and an Irishman walk into a pulpit," say the authors of *Saving Eutychus: How to preach God's word and keep people awake*. They list ten tips for preaching more clearly including: Choose the shortest, most ordinary words you can.[16] They give a website: https://readability-score.com/ where you can paste in your sermon and receive a report of how readable it is. The highest possible score is 120 (the most readable) and the Harvard Law Review has a score around 30. They suggest we should aim for a score of 70-80. (When I read this book, I was pleased to discover that my two most recent sermons received scores of 72 and 80.)

It is also important to be careful with slang. If you heard this dialogue from a man in England, what would you think? "I took the flyover on my way to the footie when I stopped to see a bloke and had a chinwag while we shared some bangers and mash. We got into a barney because he had wanted a butty. I don't know why he's so chuffed when really he's bobbins."[17] (Translation: I took the overpass on my way to the football—soccer—match when I stopped to see a man and had a conversation while we shared some sausages and mashed potatoes. We got into an argument because he had wanted a sandwich. I don't know why he is so proud when he is really a second-rate person.)

I am often surprised by what is considered American slang by British speakers. Eugene Peterson's *The Message* is disliked by some because it is so full of American slang. It communicates very well to me but not as well to others.

The slang of one English-speaking country can also be offensive in another English-speaking country. E. Randolph Richards and Brandon J. O'Brien, in their book, *Misreading Scripture with Western Eyes*, begin with this story. Richards was visiting an American friend who was teaching in Scotland and the woman driving the car was a British New Testament scholar.

> She explained that a Baptist pastor and his wife had been visiting from Georgia. As their hosting professor, she had picked them up at the airport. The pastor's wife was going to ride in the back seat so that her husband could ride up front.
>
> My British friend then stopped the story and exclaimed, "The wife opened the door, said the F-word and sat down in the seat!"
>
> I looked wide-eyed at my North American colleague. He started laughing. "You know what the F-word is, don't you?"
>
> Pastoral ministry has changed, but I still couldn't imagine a scenario in which a pastor's wife would say such a thing. I was appalled.

---

[16] Gary Millar and Phil Campbell, *Saving Eutychus: How to Preach God's Word and Keep People Awake* (Kingsford, Australia: Matthias Media, 2013), 50-61.

[17] I made up this dialogue from a list of British slang. My British friends tell me these terms are used by different social classes and would not be spoken by one person.

Our British friend was aghast. My friend continued laughing and said, "She means 'fanny.'"

Our British colleague in the front seat grimaced. "Yes. The woman said, 'I'm just going to park my'—oh that word—'right here on the seat.'" My British friend couldn't even bring herself to say "that word," since in British usage, "fanny" is impolite slang for female genitalia.[18]

ACCENTS

Pierce Pettis[19] wrote in his song, *Little River Canyon*, about growing up in Alabama, "So deep into that landscape, we did not realize / That we had been talking in accents all our lives."

In an international congregation we discover that we too have accents. When I first visited Rabat in September 1999, I met with people from different parts of the church. One morning I went to breakfast with some of the sub-Saharan African students. As I sat listening I had a difficult time understanding what was being said and asked, "What language are you speaking?" "English," they replied. It takes a while to adjust and understand African, Indian, and Korean accents, and it also takes time for people to adjust to my American accent. When students first come, they complain they can't understand me when I preach, but after a few months they are able to make the adjustment.

David and Daphne Fisher (Lisbon, Madrid) shared this illustration:

We've recently welcomed a guest pastor who will be with us for several weeks. He's been with us before, but last Sunday was the first time he spoke. I realized that I had not prepared him culturally—taking for granted that his previous two stop-overs were enough to remember some of the differences in style that he needed to assume.

He is from the southern U.S., so his accent is a little difficult for our multi-national group. He also spoke very fast which made it even worse. And, even though he didn't use any baseball or American football illustrations, his one-liners were lost on the congregation who either didn't understand them to begin with—or it's just such an American style that they didn't know it was meant to be funny! Clearly, we need to remind him of who he is speaking to!

---

[18]　E. Randolph Richards and Brandon J. O'Brien, *Misreading Scripture with Western Eyes* (Downers Grove, IL: IVP Books, 2012), 25.

[19]　Pierce Pettis is an American songwriter and lyricist. http://www.piercepettis.com/.

TRANSLATION

There was a time when we had a significant number of Spanish speakers and, more importantly, someone who was able and willing to do a simultaneous translation of the sermon. I had to get used to someone talking while I was preaching, but was glad more people would understand what I was saying. There are systems available for people to have headsets and listen to someone who translates during the service. It is not practical for us to do this since we have too many languages that would require translation so have never invested in the equipment to do that.

But I far prefer this to someone translating up front during the service where everything spoken takes twice as long. There is an art to preaching with a translator and both preacher and translator need to be good at this in order to make it effective.

PREACHING FROM A MANUSCRIPT

I admire others who can preach from just a few notes and think this has a distinct advantage for an international congregation. Most people who preach from notes use a simpler English which helps with an international congregation. There tends to be more repetition which helps deliver the point being made. And most of the people come from congregations where this is the style of the pastor's preaching.

But I have tried this and it just does not work for me. I once sat next to Mark Noll (professor of history at Notre Dame and author of several books, including *The Scandal of the Evangelical Mind*) at a wedding. We talked about preaching and he also preaches from a manuscript. He told me that he goes to a lot of trouble to choose the right word and the right phrase to say exactly what he wants to say and why, after going to all that trouble, would he throw it away and speak from notes? I resonated with this.

There are advantages to preaching from a manuscript. For one, I can print out extra copies to give to people who struggle with English so they can follow me with a written copy as I preach. I talked with an international pastor who has a sizable number of Asians in his congregation and although he is capable of preaching from notes, he disciplines himself to preach from a manuscript—and stick to it—so that these Asians can follow with a printed copy of his sermon. If there is someone doing simultaneous translation, a manuscript will make that task much easier.

Another benefit of preaching from a manuscript is that the preacher is able to choose words more carefully. Slang can be avoided. It takes time for people not used to someone preaching from a manuscript to make the necessary adjustment but I think the positives of preaching from a manuscript are significant enough to make it worth trying.

The authors of *Saving Eutychus* both preach from a manuscript and offer tips to improve delivery of the sermon. They make the point that "if you master the art of *natural scripting*—writing exactly the words you'd naturally speak, exactly the way you'd say them—then you can eliminate the downsides of scripted public speaking."[20]

I also put up PowerPoint slides as I preach. This is especially helpful when I quote Scripture (which is quite a lot) or read a quote from someone. When we combine two or more of our senses, communication becomes more clear. So the audio and visual combination is very helpful.

CULTURAL POINTS OF VIEW

I once took a business trip to Japan and prepared by studying what should and should not be done by foreigners. I learned how to present a business card, how to greet someone, and how to leave wine in my glass to indicate I was finished. But in a congregation with thirty-five or more nationalities, a pastor needs help negotiating through all the various cultures and expectations.

I have had the sad experience of preaching at two funerals for students who had come from Ghana for their university studies in Morocco. When I was preparing the funeral service for the second of these students, a Ghanaian friend pointed out to me that it would not be helpful for me to be explicit about the cause of death (which was cancer) as I had done in the first funeral service. It was not that it was shameful, but simply that in Ghanaian culture it is not appropriate to talk about death so explicitly.

There are cultural ways of relating to the pastor. In African cultures, the pastor is elevated and the people of the church serve the pastor. When I arrive at church and begin to get out of the car, if there are Africans there, they will want to help me carry my guitar, my backpack, anything I have. I resist this and say I can carry things myself. I am trying not to be like a colonialist and instead be a servant, but this can be viewed as a rejection of their desire to honor me.

Pastors from the U.S. tend to dress informally but this is viewed negatively by sub-Saharan Africans and Asians who expect the pastor to dress up on Sunday.

---

[20] Millar and Cambell, *Saving Eutychus*, 45.

I have learned that when you are given a present, or are giving a present, it is important to know if this is a culture where the present is opened in front of everyone or taken home and opened later. To choose the wrong option is to be unintentionally offensive.

When a Korean compliments me on a sermon, "Nice message today," and I respond by saying, "Thank you," my response will be viewed as arrogant and proud. The proper response in Korean culture is to say something that is self-deprecating. Humility needs to be shown.

In South Africa, Christians kiss each other on the lips when they meet in church. In Africa you hug but do not kiss. In Morocco, expatriates follow the European culture and kiss once on each cheek. Moroccans kiss at least once on each cheek, many times two or three times on each cheek. Men do this with men. (It is a bit strange for me to kiss someone with a beard.)

Once again, it is very helpful to have people from other cultures to act as sounding boards to help you communicate more clearly.

Ken MacHarg (Latin America, Europe, Central Asia) gives this illustration:

> Cultural cues are so important. After serving as a missionary and occasionally as the pastor of an international church in Latin America for over 20 years where the people are touchy and kissy, I had a difficult transfer to Central Asia where you don't touch anyone, and especially a man does not even shake hands with a woman. I actually had to keep my hands in my pockets to prevent myself from trying to shake the hand of a woman.

Steve McMichael (Tangier, Zambia) gives this illustration:

> World view creates problems, particularly among international staff. Our church staff included several Americans and a Zambian pastor. One Wednesday night the Zambian associate pastor was doing announcements and began to "freelance" about how France had forgiven 6 million euros of Zambian debt. What began as a praise report quickly veered into a scathing rebuke of the white man's wickedness in charging interest and again praise to God for correcting them. After this catharsis, he realized his next responsibility was to introduce the white man who was speaking that evening. . . . it was awkward, but a great lesson in how we all need to continually evaluate our world views and how they influence our thinking towards others.

WORLD VIEWS

One of the major differences in a multicultural church is the different world views that are foundational to the way people understand the Bible and live a Christian life.

Roland Müller wrote a book, *The Messenger, the Message, the Community: Three Critical Issues for the Cross-Cultural Church-Planter.* In the middle part of the book, "The Message," he writes of three world views. There is the guilt/innocence world view of North America and Europe. This world view focuses on being right and wrong. The conscience figures prominently in this world view. When those with this world view read the Bible, they see a gospel that says we are sinners and are guilty because of our sin. God has a sense of justice that must be satisfied so we can be redeemed.

North Africa, the Middle East, and Asia have an honor/shame world view. In this world view it is not as important to be right as it is to protect your honor.

Arabs tell a story of a sheik who was sleeping under a palm tree. While he was sleeping, a thief stole his expensive cloak. The family of the sheik hunted down the thief and brought him to trial. At the trial the thief said, "Yes I did steal this cloak. I found a man lying under a palm tree and had sexual relations with him before I took his cloak." The sheik immediately asked to see the cloak, took a quick look at it and said, "This is not my cloak," and the thief was set free.[21]

The honor of the sheik was more important than the theft of his cloak. In the guilt/innocence culture of the West, the man would have said, "He's lying. That is my cloak and I would have known if he had sexual relations with me but he did not. Convict him. He's guilty." In the West justice is more important than honor. In honor/shame cultures, honor must be protected at all costs. The gospel story is a story of the restoration of honor.

The third world view is the fear/power world view found in sub-Saharan Africa and some island tribal groups. This world view is very sensitive to the supernatural world of angels and spirits and demons. The gospel is a demonstration of God's power over forces of darkness.

Cultures reflect not just one of these world views but one dominates in the culture. Morocco is primarily an honor/shame culture but it is also a fear/power culture.

All three world views are reflected in the Bible. In the creation story in Genesis, for example, when Adam and Eve sinned in the garden of Eden,

---

[21] Roland Muller, *The Messenger, the Message, the Community: Three Critical Issues for the Cross-Cultural Church-Planter* (Altona, Canada: CanBooks, 2006), 16.

they disobeyed God and moved from their innocence to being guilty of sin. They moved from being naked and feeling no shame to having to cover their nakedness because of shame. They went from walking with God in the garden to hiding because they were afraid. The consequence of the fall was that they experienced guilt, shame, and fear.

If I approach the stories of the Bible with only the guilt/innocence world view of the West, not only will I miss the opportunity to communicate the truths of Scripture more clearly to those from other parts of the world, I will also miss some of the powerful truths of Scripture for myself.

Because the honor/shame world view of North Africa and the Middle East was the world view of the Palestine of Jesus, when we read the Gospels and Acts through that filter the stories become more clear and speak more powerfully. Let me give an example.

The parable of "The Workers in the Vineyard" is found in Matthew 20:1–16. The landowner came out early in the morning to hire workers for the day and agreed to pay them a day's wage, one denarius. He went back at 9 a.m. and hired more workers, agreeing to pay them fairly. He went back at noon and 3 p.m. and at 5 p.m., hiring more workers each time. At the end of the day, at 6 p.m., he began to pay the workers, starting with the ones who were hired last. When those who had only worked an hour received one denarius, those who had worked most or all of the day began to be excited, thinking of all they would receive. But each person, regardless of how long he had worked, received one denarius, a day's wage. When those who had worked the whole day protested, the landowner said he had the right to do with his money what he wanted.

The lesson we from the West with our guilt/innocence world view take from this parable is the equality of God's grace. We all receive from God. But when you read this parable from the perspective of an honor/shame world view, there is a very different and more powerful truth that is expressed.

Here in Morocco when I go to the market, I walk past a row of men who are sitting on the side of the road waiting to be hired. They sit with the tools of their trade in front of them: plumbing, carpentry, masonry. Some are hired at the beginning of the day but the rest sit all day, waiting. And as they wait, they are exposed to the public view. People passing by see who is hired early in the day and who waits all day without being hired. They see who is hired most days and who sits there most days.

There is a public shaming of those who are not hired, not wanted. When the landowner came and hired men at the end of the day, he restored honor because at least they were wanted. When he paid them as much as he paid those who had worked all day, he gave them money they needed, but more importantly, he restored their honor.

This parable speaks powerfully to those in the world who are rejected, despised, unwanted, left in the wake of the rich and powerful of the world. The coming of the kingdom of God into their lives is a restoration of honor.

If a pastor of an international church takes time to read the Bible through the eyes of differing world views, the international congregation will benefit, as will the pastor.

Another way different world views impact preaching is how we view the devil and spiritual warfare. The challenge in the West is to believe that the devil exists. But Africans have no doubt about the existence of the devil and have experience after experience with the power of witchcraft. When I have preached about resisting the devil, I have had to speak to both world views.

Our different world views explain why Africans have all-night prayer meetings,[22] while Westerners think they are on a marathon of prayer if they pray for more than an hour. The night is when forces of evil are most present and so all-night prayer combats forces of evil in the darkness of night.

The New Faces of Christianity: Believing the Bible in the Global South by Philip Jenkins offers great insights into how the fear/power world view of Africa affects Christian behavior and I found myself saying, as I read the book, "Oh, that's why they do this."

TRANSITION

An international church with its high rate of transition does not have the luxury of preaching a foundation of truth and then building on it over time. A third or more of the congregation this fall will not have heard the sermons I preached last fall. What do I do if I want the congregation to understand how I view financial stewardship? Am I supposed to preach that sermon every three to six months?

For this reason, I prefer to preach through books of the Bible. When I preach topically, I am trying to address a need I perceive in the congregation. But when I preach through a book of the Bible, I am taken to places I would not normally go. I end up preaching on a wider range of topics than I would if I were choosing the topics myself. This also helps to push past my denominational

---

[22]   "A belief in confrontation with dark forces helps explain the practice of vigils and all-night services, which are commonplace throughout African and Asian churches"; Philip Jenkins, *The New Faces of Christianity: Believing the Bible in the Global South* (New York: Oxford University, 2008), 109.

background and I preach sermons about healing and casting out demons because that is what the text says Jesus and his disciples did.

In recent years, I have preached from Romans starting the first Sunday in January. I continue up to Lent and then preach from the Gospels through Easter. Then I preach from Acts up into the summer. The summer varies. Sometimes I have preached from the Psalms, but in the fall, starting in September, I preach from the Old Testament up to Advent when I preach on the birth of Jesus and his promised return.

I think this is a healthy spiritual diet for the church. After 12 winters of Romans I switched to James. Now I am preaching from Ephesians. One of the benefits for me is that I fall in love with the books of the Bible from which I preach. People come and go and few are able to join me for the whole series, but I am enriched and I regret that I will not live long enough to preach through all the books of the Bible.

THEOLOGICAL SENSITIVITY

Denominational distinctives separate the body of Christ. In our view of sacraments (some call them ordinances), Protestants are agreed on the number, two: baptism and communion. But what happens during those sacraments? Is the taking of bread and wine (or juice) merely a symbol, or is there a spiritual presence in those elements? Is baptism valid only if immersed as an adult? Can an infant by baptized by sprinkling?

Christians normally don't get in many arguments about this because we divide into different church denominations where everyone is in agreement. But what happens when all these different denominations meet in the same place of worship? What happens when a woman preaches? What happens when we talk about the gifts of the Spirit? There are many contentious theological differences and it is a challenge to have representatives from each side of these issues in one church.

What is not helpful is to water down what you believe until you say nothing, offend no one, and bore everyone, including yourself. One pastor described the theology of an international church this way: "Defining the theology of this church is like pinning Jell-O to the wall."[23] This is not what we want; we need to preach the truth with passion. But in preaching what you believe to be true, it is important to carry peripheral issues with a sense of humility. We need to preach with passion from the core of what we believe and

---

[23]   Pederson, *Expatriate Ministry*, 53.

preach with a greater sense of humility on the denominational distinctives. The core should dominate in preaching with the denominational distinctives taking a distant second place.

Mark DeYmaz comments:

Of course, in any church, it is important to clarify what you believe. But for those pursuing the multi-ethnic church, it is essential. For with diverse people comes diverse theology; consequently, multi-ethnic church leaders must be up-front and clear about the beliefs of the church in order to "keep the unity of the Spirit through the bond of peace" (Eph. 4:3). We should never compromise our convictions for the sake of diversity. One way to be proactive in this regard is to post a doctrinal statement on your website or in some other visible location within the church. I recommend, however, that it speak only about the essential doctrines of the Christian faith, allowing room to accommodate various views on the more nonessential positions of teaching that you will certainly encounter from those seeking to join a multi-ethnic church. Resist the urge to speak to every possible issue in your doctrinal statement, and beyond this, do not be afraid of divergent opinions concerning the nonessentials. As long as those who hold them do not become divisive—by seeking to impose their views on others or by failing to consider others as more important than themselves in the practice of their faith—the healthy dialogue and the exchange of experiential understanding will invite and inspire spiritual growth within the body.[24]

David Packer (Singapore, Stuttgart) comments:

I usually say something to people like this: "We do not feel bad about being Baptists. We do not apologize for our beliefs, but we also don't try to hit everybody over the head with them either. We focus on what we have in common, on the more important elements of our faith. And we try to relate to one another graciously." And then I add that my daughter is a Presbyterian minister and that tends to make everybody feel better.

[24]   Mark DeYmaz & Harry Li, *Ethnic Blends: Mixing Diversity into Your Local Church* (Grand Rapids, MI; Zondervan, 2010), 86-87.

CORE ISSUES

In the appendix I cover several theological issues in more depth. Core issues is one of these and I encourage you to take time to read through the appendix. I promise you that it is not overly academic.

As a pastor of an international church with many different denominational backgrounds, it is important not to be dogmatic. We need to hold on to the core and be flexible on the denominational distinctives. But what are the core issues of the Christian faith? What beliefs are peripheral and which are essential?

Every denomination has what it considers to be the core of faith, but when you place them side by side, there are significant differences. I argue that to find the core, it is necessary to find agreement between Evangelicals and Pentecostals. Where they agree, we find the core. Where they disagree, we find what I call denominational distinctives.

When we spend a lot of time preaching on the denominational distinctives, we unnecessarily divide the church. When we spend time preaching on the core of our faith, we build the faith and unity of the church.

One of the strengths of an international church, especially one that has a great diversity because there are no other options, is that we gradually pick away the peripheral doctrines until we are left with the beautiful core. This is not in any way a reduction of what we believe. As we each push to the side our peripheral doctrine, each of us illuminates the part of the core our denominational perspective has magnified. As a consequence, together we help each other to see a more complete, greater core than we had seen before.

Holy Spirit

When I was preaching through the book of Acts, I preached from passages that are used in the argument between Pentecostals and dispensationalists. One side teaches that we need to experience a second baptism of the Holy Spirit; the other side teaches that the "spectacular gifts" ceased with the apostles. My approach was to paint what I view as the two extremes and then pull people to the center, which is where I believe the unifying truth is found. I talked about our need to be filled with the Holy Spirit and our need to be continually filled with the Holy Spirit. I talked about a willingness to receive from God any gift he wanted us to have and the folly of telling God we will accept this gift but not that one. This is where I find we can be unified.

Baptism (Water Baptism)

In my fifteen years as pastor of RIC, I have never baptized an infant. In my five and a half years as a Presbyterian pastor, I did not baptize anyone who was not an infant. Here in Morocco I have baptized in bathtubs and plastic pools, but most of the time we baptize people in the ocean. We gather at the beach, and the person to be baptized tells us his or her story of coming to faith and deciding to be baptized. We wade out into deeper water, and as the person goes under the water (I have learned to time going under the water with the arrival of a wave), I remind them they are dead to sin. As they come up I tell them they are alive in Christ. I love the aesthetics and symbolism of this act of baptism. It is a beautiful reflection of what happens to us spiritually.

There was one couple who came to me and wanted their infant son baptized. They were from the Philippines and I talked with them about the options before them: baptism or dedication. They seemed unclear about which to choose so I asked them what the church they were returning to did, which option would fit in better with the culture of that church. They told me most people there were baptized as adults and so we decided to dedicate their son to Jesus.

To baptize an infant in our church would cause a lot of people, especially those from sub-Saharan Africa, to wonder what was going on. If the couple had chosen to have their infant son baptized, I would have preached a sermon on baptism, explaining the two sides to the debate, and reminding the congregation that this was not a core issue that should separate us. If you are unwilling to baptize an infant when that is requested, you need to be able to give permission for someone else to do that in the international church you serve.

Creationism—Intelligent Design—Theistic Evolution

I think the Christian community does itself a disservice by holding on to a young earth, seven-day creation. To ignore the strong scientific evidence of evolution and to replace that science with pseudo-science discredits whatever else these Christians believe.

I believe the church is going through the same pain it did when Copernicus challenged the church's teaching that the earth was the center of the universe by showing the earth revolved around the sun. It took many years for the church to adjust to the clear scientific evidence. Frances Collins, who headed up the Human Genome Project, wrote, *The Language of God: A Scientist Presents Evidence for Belief.* In this book he presents a critique of atheism, agnosticism, creationism, and intelligent design. He then presents what has been learned from the study of genetics and talks about what he observes that affirms his faith in God.

This is a very unsettling belief for some people in the church and I have gotten into trouble when teaching through Genesis and making my view known. So since that time, when I teach or preach, what I emphasize is that God created. Whether people believe God created in seven days, a short seven thousand years ago, or God created through the process of evolution over millions and billions of years, the point is that God created.

Women Preaching

We have had women preaching over the years I have been pastor at RIC and it has not been an issue. I am told that one couple would skip church on the Sunday a woman was going to preach but I never noticed it. (I suspect people are more tolerant in international churches than they are in their home churches.) Some people I have talked with about this distinguish between a woman preaching and a woman leading as a pastor.

I have not had the need to preach about this yet, but if I was going to preach through 1 Timothy, for example, and came to 1 Timothy 2:11–15:

> A woman should learn in quietness and full submission. I do not permit a woman to teach or to have authority over a man; she must be silent. For Adam was formed first, then Eve. And Adam was not the one deceived; it was the woman who was deceived and became a sinner. But women will be saved through childbearing—if they continue in faith, love and holiness with propriety.

I think I would have to point out the inconsistency between how we interpret this passage and Paul's letters when he commends women who are preaching and leading in churches. I would have to say that, because this is an issue about which followers of Jesus differ, it is not a core issue and we should not divide over it. Of all the things we can do that offend God, this is surely way down on that list.

Daphne Fisher (Lisbon, Madrid) gives this illustration:

> In our very young church in Madrid, we began to form an elder team. Our missionary team leader asked me to be on this team—he specifically wanted a woman on the Elder board. I had been teaching at our Sunday worship with some frequency already and in my home church there are women elders so this was comfortable for me.

However, it was not as comfortable for others. Two families approached our team leader to voice their concerns. Neither family had objected when I taught, but to have a woman elder seemed to cross the line. But in truth, I was more than an elder. When our team leader had asked the four of us elders who was willing to be the "head elder"—the three men literally took a step back, leaving me the only one willing.

Our agreement was that I would take this role only for six months and then one of the men would rotate in. In fact, head elder would be a rotating responsibility. But when it was announced that I, a woman, was head elder, these two couples objected.

We were sent various emails from one man, citing all the Scriptures that might have anything remotely related to the subject of women in authority. We were clearly told that attempting to distort the clearly stated truth in Scripture by appealing to the Hebrew or Greek or culture context was NOT acceptable—so don't even try it.

The irony to me was that this particular man had often emailed me after I spoke to commend me. Now I wondered if that had been more of a way to assert his voice over mine. After a couple of meetings with our team leader, this man, his wife, and three daughters left our church.

The other family also talked with our team leader—and with me. No emails. They said that had we listed the elders on the website—which was how they discovered our church—they would never have come in the first place. However, they came to the decision that since there wasn't an alternative church they could conveniently go to and they loved our community, they would respectfully and lovingly agree to disagree. They continued to attend and participate like before.

Two months later, they received a newsletter from their home church announcing a new perspective of the role of women in ministry! Their home church, which had formed their opinion about this, had changed their understanding and were now embracing women's roles in ministry!

Communion

Our practice at RIC is to have people come to the front of the church, take the bread, dip it into the juice, and then eat it. When I introduce communion, I invite anyone who loves Jesus and is seeking to follow him in obedience to come forward. I tell parents that it is up to them if their child takes communion or not and tell them that if they prefer their child to be prayed for, to let us know and we will bless their child as they come.

It does bother me when I see a parent bring their very young child and show them how to dip the bread into the cup and eat it. I would prefer that children be older, but with so many denominational backgrounds it is not appropriate for me to enforce my Presbyterian understanding of communion on everyone. We have to be flexible.

For most of my years we have used grape juice for communion. There was one Sunday when we had forgotten to buy grape juice and a Korean pastor gave me a bottle of Jerusalem wine to use. We used wine for a short period of time and then reverted back to grape juice. This did not create a problem in the church.

Use of Alcohol

One Sunday when I preached from Ecclesiastes and the pursuit of pleasure, I began with a long list of things I find pleasurable, including food. Among these, a German meal of salty chicken and spicy french fries was followed by a cold German beer. And a plate of French cheese, crackers, and melon was enjoyed with a glass of wine. One of the members of the church was upset that I had referenced drinking wine and beer and I apologized. I try not to reference the use of alcohol in my preaching or church communications. But I also pointed out that the prohibition of alcohol is not biblical. We are not supposed to get drunk but the Bible is clear that drinking alcohol is part of the blessing God has given us.[25]

I also pointed out in a sermon from Romans 14 where Paul talks about not causing a weaker brother to stumble that the goal is not to become the weaker brother and manipulatively use Paul's teaching to strengthen your personal belief.

I fully understand why parts of the church reacted to the abuse of alcohol in the U.S. Families were being destroyed by this abuse. My only problem is that they tried to make the prohibition of alcohol a biblical issue. We abuse sex but do not get rid of sex. We abuse food but do not get rid of food.

The prohibition of alcohol as part of Christian living is more of an American issue (as well as African and Asian congregations influenced by American missionaries). In a congregation of internationals, it is not appropriate to

---

[25] Wine was presented in the Temple in Jerusalem as a drink offering. The Law instructed Israel to take a tithe and use it to "buy whatever you like: cattle, sheep, wine or other fermented drink, or anything you wish. Then you and your household shall eat there in the presence of the LORD your God and rejoice." Deuteronomy 14:26.

impose an American understanding on those from other countries.[26] We do offer both wine and grape juice during our annual Seder meal. This has not been an issue in our church.

Christians in Europe accept drinking alcohol as a natural part of their culture. I was in France, studying French in a class of seven other Americans. The professor spoke about French hospitality and how important it was to select the proper wine for the meal. He said it would be impolite not to drink a glass. There were two couples from a tradition that does not permit drinking alcohol and they were uncomfortable with this. So I suggested that if Jesus had enough faith to turn water into wine, they should have enough faith to drink the wine and have it changed to water. They were not impressed.

David Packer (Singapore, Stuttgart) gives this illustration:

> A story was told of a Baptist layman from the state of Kentucky who visited a missionary his church supported in Italy in the 1950s. The missionary's Italian church hosted a party for the American guest, but during the party the Kentuckian slipped outside to smoke a cigarette—Kentucky is a state where tobacco is widely grown and in the 1950s many Baptists smoked. The Italian host went out to check on him and she was so shocked to see him smoking a cigarette that she dropped her glass of wine![27]

David and Daphne Fisher (Lisbon, Madrid) comment:

> Some of our colleagues in ministry come from conservative church homes. The "freedom" they've found to be culturally engaged with wine or beer would been seen as a problem. So, it's not unusual in this day of Facebook to be asked to remove the bottles or glasses from the photo about to be taken—or just not post it on Facebook!

Millennial Points of View

If anyone ever asks me about my millennial view, I tell them that as soon as I master the fruit of the Spirit, I will consider my millennial view. And anyone who

---

[26]   The American Assemblies of God pastors do not drink alcohol, but the French Assemblies of God pastors do. One AoG church in France announced one Sunday that the next week an American AoG pastor would be visiting and speaking, so in deference to him they should not bring wine for the meal that followed church each week. The next Sunday everyone, except for the French pastor, came with thermoses of wine so it was not obvious what they were drinking.

[27]   Packer, *Look Who God Let into the Church*, 180.

knows me understands this will be a long way off. It is so distressing to me that Christians are divided by our speculation about what will happen in the future.

We are not any smarter than scholars 2,000 years ago. We have more information, but we are not smarter. The great minds two millennia ago considered when the Messiah would come and how it would be. They were confident in what they understood the Scriptures to be saying and yet they were wrong. It seems to me that there is an arrogance in thinking we are so smart we can have it all figured out this time, how the end will be, and what the return of Jesus will be like.

A pastor who places an emphasis on any of these non-core issues will work against the health of an international, multidenominational church. It is okay to have an opinion, but when it is shared, it needs to be shared with a sense of humility.

SHARING THE PULPIT

Every preacher has his or her own favorite topics and themes. Because of this, it is helpful to have others preach regularly. I like the pattern of preaching three Sundays and then having someone else preach the fourth Sunday. This provides the congregation with a variety in their spiritual diet.

An international church is often blessed by having a number of people with the gift of preaching. Offering them the opportunity to preach is helpful because they are able to use their gift and helpful because the congregation sees one of their own sharing what God has been teaching them. When I sense that someone might have the gift of preaching, I encourage them to try it out, usually during one of the summer Sundays.

However, it is not helpful to allow just anyone in the congregation to preach because there will be people who want to preach but have a theology I consider destructive. In my early years, I allowed myself to be talked into allowing one of the sub-Saharan African migrants to preach during one of the summer Sundays. His sermon was heretical with its message of the health and wealth gospel. The only consolation was that because of his accent, half of the congregation could not understand what he was saying.

The pastor of a church has a responsibility to protect the flock from bad theology and discernment is needed. Periodically I receive an email from someone telling me they have a "powerful ministry of healing and deliverance," and would like to come to our church. My response is that if they have such a powerful ministry and if it truly is of God, then they have no need to promote themselves. I pray for an outpouring of the Holy Spirit in this nation, but I want it to come from God and not human efforts to promote the speaker. I don't want to block what God wants to bring to us, but I also want to protect the flock God has given me.

TEACHING

RAPIDLY CHANGING DEMOGRAPHICS

Our Sunday School program ends sometime between the end of May and the middle of June, depending on when those who are leading Sunday School leave for vacation or move to a new assignment. When September comes, we can have a completely different Sunday School.

One year we ended in May with a Sunday School of seventeen children and youth. (That is youth singular. There was one high school girl in the church.) Starting in September we had forty-eight in the Sunday School, including enough youth to have both a junior high and a senior high group.

Over the years, we never had more than five or six infants in our nursery until September 2012 when we suddenly discovered we had seventeen children under the age of four.

The demographics of our church can change radically over the summer. This poses some challenges and one of them is finding teachers for the classes. It is not simply a matter of finding extra teachers to expand Sunday School from seventeen to forty-eight, the challenge is complicated by teachers themselves moving away each summer.

In 2012, every teacher, except for three helpers, moved away in June or July. We faced Sunday School in September with no teachers and had to wait patiently for new people to arrive and discover who would be willing to teach a class. This is a bit nerve-wracking and over the years I have learned that it does no good to worry. I have learned to relax and wait because each year new teachers arise. Part of my job, after fifteen years of experience, is to continually reassure people that we will be all right in September. When there is an influx of children and youth, parents come with them and among them we find teachers.

This presents another challenge: how do you vet teachers to be sure they will be able to teach effectively? The truth is that you have to take a risk and sometimes mistakes will be made. We don't have the luxury of getting to know someone for a year or even three months before asking if they would like to teach Sunday School. We often have no more than a month or a couple weeks before we have to make that decision.

We try to get to know people when they arrive in the summer and gauge whether or not they would be good teachers for the children in the church. As much as possible, we have them assist another teacher to give us more time to get to know them and see how well they would do on their own but sometimes that is not possible. Malcolm Gladwell wrote in his book, *Blink,* that we are capable of making instantaneous judgments, and we do a pretty good job of that, but there have been a few times when we had to step in and help someone understand that it would not be good for them to continue as teachers.

FLEXIBILITY IN PROGRAMS

With the potential for massive change each September, flexibility is key. It does not help to have a rigidly set program into which people must fit. It is good to have a program in place, but when someone comes in with a strong sense of what they want to do, I have found it is best to make adjustments. About five years ago, a couple arrived over the summer and volunteered to take over the Sunday School program. They were active with Awana, a program I was not familiar with. But I agreed and they had materials sent in. This program was very successful. Parents and children loved it and after a couple years, when they left, another couple took it over. When that couple left we had difficulty finding someone to continue it but kept it going. This fall we will transition to another Sunday School curriculum. A new couple has agreed to take over Sunday School and we are going with materials they are more comfortable with. It is important that new teachers be encouraged and a rigidly fixed program makes this more difficult.

ADULT SUNDAY SCHOOL

Sunday School as an adult activity is not universal. For many cultures, church lasts for three or more hours and Sunday School is for children. Adult Sunday School sounds like an oxymoron. We have to work hard to encourage adults to take advantage of classes.

I am continually looking around at people new to the church to see who might be a good teacher for adults. We have had rich teaching experiences with scholars doing research in Morocco.

SHORT SERIES

In a transitional church, we have discovered it is most effective to have short series of teaching. Recently a man in the church has been burdened with a desire to pray more intently and has taken time to fast and pray and reflect. He taught a three-night class on intercession that was very helpful to many of us in the church. So we encourage people in the church to share with others what they are learning from God. This way more people can commit to a short-term course, grow in knowledge and understanding, and have a feeling of satisfaction about completing the course.

David and Daphne Fisher (Lisbon, Madrid) share this story:

> We have a struggle to meet more than six weeks in a row. I cannot think of one time that a small group has met that long without people missing. It makes most study series very challenging and the group connection difficult. However, we have nonetheless had some great on-going groups and since everyone is so understanding of their popping in and out culture, they carry on and do their best. We've found that a seminar is sometimes helpful—but that doesn't really contribute to the group bonding.

Barry Gaeddert (London) comments:

> At ICC, I always saw our job (and taught the staff, the lay leadership, and the congregation for that matter) to train people to go in to the world. They were with us for one year, or two or three years. And then they often went to places around the globe. So our job was to invest spiritually, help them grow in their walk with God, to learn about their gifts and how to use them . . . and then to send them on more mature than when they arrived. We were to be faithful to teach, train, and encourage people for whatever period of time they were with us. This does not match the "spiritual maturity" programs that are prevalent in large mega-churches in the US, where people spend years working through a program. Our job is to take them as we get them and help them grow until they are sent elsewhere!

John Carlock (Cairo) shares this story:

> We had a small group leader who was married to a Korean and had spent a number of years in a church in Korea where he was involved in small groups in a fairly large church. He had a book that he had read that was typical of the small groups we have in the United States and that is used in large churches in Korea. The idea was that you needed twenty to thirty people in the small group. It was semester based so you did not want people coming and going once the groups had started. If anyone wanted to come into the group in the middle of the semester, this was not advisable. So these were closed groups.

In the Korean setting, at the end of the semester, as these groups grow, new groups could break off and multiplication would take place in the church. The problem with that is in Cairo we have people coming and going constantly. So as new people come we try to get them into small groups right away whether or not the small group is in the middle of the semester. Because people are leaving the same time as people are coming, it is difficult to get a consistent number of people in a small group. We normally have eight to twelve in a small group. There may be one or two who leave during the semester and one or two who join. So the dynamic is not the same as what we have in the states or what he had experienced in Korea. So I encouraged him to build relationships with small group leaders, not to worry so much about structure, make the groups open and available, allow people to come and go freely, and build a sense of community in that small group.

MEN'S BIBLE STUDY

When I arrived, there was an early morning men's Bible Study and they were going through the Chuck Swindol Bible character studies. This lasted for a few years but then those who were active moved away and other men in the church did not seem very interested. I tried several times to restart this study over the years, but nothing happened. I met with individual men but there was no group meeting.

Then, a few years ago, with a different population, there was interest and we began a Saturday morning study which worked well until the percentage of men in the group with small children increased. The wives of these men were not happy to have their husbands absent on Saturday mornings when they wanted help with the children, so it dwindled to three or four of us who did not have small children. I was slow to deal with this but finally we switched to a Wednesday lunch Bible study and this is working well. Once again, flexibility and an awareness of changing needs is important.

WORSHIP

The goal of worship in a church is to lift up praise to Jesus and to help open hearts and minds to hear God speak through the Word read and preached, not to preserve any particular worship style.

The tension between those who want to sing hymns and those who prefer contemporary songs exists in many churches in the world, but the diversity of an international church accentuates the tension. In an Episcopal church, there might be a debate about what songs to sing but there is an agreed-on liturgy that is followed. National churches can be high church or low church. They can be Pentecostal or Evangelical. But they are one or the other. In an international church, and especially international churches where there are no other options, all these traditions become mixed together.

So we have Catholics, Anglicans, Episcopalians, and down the liturgical line to Baptists, Pentecostals, Quakers, and Mennonites. On the theological scale we have Pentecostals and dispensationalists. We have Evangelicals and those who come from mainline denominations. We have so many different sets of expectations of what a church should be like that I like to joke that if everyone leaves equally dissatisfied, we have done a good job. The point is that for most people, we are likely to be a different church than the one they are used to.

FLEXIBILITY IN WORSHIP

So how do we handle this diversity? We can choose to have a style to which we expect people to adapt, or, because we have people who come from so many backgrounds, we can value the very rich pool from which we can draw. To choose the first is to make those not used to that style continually uncomfortable. To choose the second helps people to embrace the different styles and celebrate diversity.

In our highly transitional church, those who lead worship come and go. As a result, sometimes our worship has had more of a Pentecostal flavor and at other times, more of an Evangelical flavor. Our current music team has a blend of African-style worship and Caribbean-style worship blended with contemporary worship. This is part of what makes RIC such a rich church.

I have observed, over the years, that those who are more spiritually mature are able to benefit from different styles of worship. Those who have a more cultural spirituality are usually more critical. There was one couple who had been part of a church in Peru where a friend of mine met them. He told them about me and our church and I expected them to be active members when they arrived in Rabat. But when they discovered we had a more contemporary worship service, they began to come to church halfway through the service so they would miss the worship and be there just for the sermon. Their inability to adjust caused them to miss a great opportunity.

OPENNESS TO NEW FORMS OF WORSHIP

I am not a fan of dance, so when a woman from South Africa wanted to do liturgical dance at RIC, I agreed only because I knew other people liked this.

And then, to my surprise, I discovered that this dance spoke to me in a powerful way, bypassing my brain and going straight to my heart. Since then I have loved the dancing of a woman from Jamaica, the choreographed dances of a talented group of Caribbeans and Africans, and more recently the beautiful, colorful, swaying dance of students from the South Pacific island of Tuvalu.

A mime from Argentina led in our worship many times. I remember coming back from a summer of language study in France, listening to Graham Kendrick's new album, *What Grace*, and wishing we could sing some of these songs in our church. My first Sunday back, this man did a mime to Kendrick's "I Kneel Down." It was beautiful. This man also led us in a mime he did at our Easter sunrise service that stands out as a highlight for me.

One of the more interesting concerts we had was an Easter concert where a choir had prepared portions of Handel's *Messiah*. Interspersed in this was a Taekwondo presentation of the gospel. A South Korean had started classes for Taekwondo and his students stood on the stage and one by one broke boards labeled anger, gossip, pride, etc. They did this with their hands and their feet. Then a visiting, five-black-belt Korean came up. A wicker basket was raised on a pole, about fifteen feet in the air. The basket was labeled sin. The man bowed to us, turned around, ran to the back of the stage, put his foot on the wall, and did a flip in the air, kicking the heck out of the basket which was filled with confetti that flew out into the front rows of the church. He turned to us, bowed, and we gave him a standing ovation. Following this the choir came out and we continued singing Handel's *Messiah*. Afterward, I talked with the Korean ambassador who explained to me that Taekwondo is the national sport in South Korea and that these demonstrations are part of church services in South Korea.

EMBRACING OTHER CULTURES

We love the diversity of our church and celebrate it. One of the best times to do this is during Advent. We open our services with the lighting of the advent wreath and each week we invite one of the national groups of the church to lead us. What they do varies, but typically the Christmas story scripture for that day is read in their native language (we print the passage in English in the bulletin so people can follow along), they sing a traditional Christmas song from their country, and they pray for us in their language. During our Christmas Eve program, we sing *Silent Night* in as many languages as possible.

Sometimes we read Luke 2:10–11, "But the angel said to them, 'Do not be afraid. I bring you good news of great joy that will be for all the people. Today in the town of David a Savior has been born to you; he is Christ the Lord,'" and invite people to come up and say "I bring you good news of great joy" in their own language. To hear this declaration of good news in twenty languages is very powerful.

What we experience is a little bit of what I imagine heaven will be like with God's children, from all of time, gathering to give praise to God with all the beauty of the diverse cultures represented. I would love to see what Rich Mullins and Johann Sebastian Bach come up with in a collaborative effort. It will be exciting and here in Rabat we are blessed to get a taste of what is to come.

VISITING TEAMS

An international church attracts people looking for a place to minister and this can sometimes be nothing more than a need to showcase their talents, add another country to their list, or justify their travels. I receive emails from people wanting to visit Morocco to minister in our church with their gift of banners, pageantry, dance, and so on. I have learned to be cautious before saying yes and I will check out the person or group on the Internet as well as talk with other international church pastors about the invitation. We enjoy celebrating our diversity but we need to be careful as well about who we invite to lead in our services.

We have been blessed many times with visiting teams and I want to be open to those God sends, but I also have a responsibility to protect the flock God has put in my charge. It is a difficult balance.

Ken MacHarg (Latin America, Europe, Central Asia) gives this illustration:

> I note your questions about those who want to visit and serve in Rabat. I have become very conscious of this here in Prague. I received enough offers to "come and serve your church" this past summer that I could have had a traveling preacher/music leader, etc. almost every Sunday. What made me very skeptical has been that all of the offers involve the summer months (nobody wants to come to Prague in the winter!), and were sometimes part of "God's call to us to make an eight city tour of Europe in which we would sing and/or preach." During three summers that I served in Kyrgyzstan (where is Kyrgyzstan? How do you spell that? A Muslim country? It's a long way away, isn't it?) I never had one offer!

ADAPTING TO VARYING LEVELS OF SKILL

At times we have had skilled musicians leading worship and at other times the church has had to put up with just me and my guitar. For a period of time we had a professional pianist who played for us and we took advantage of the opportunity to play some songs that were more demanding musically. In the last five years we have had a man from Ghana who is a skilled musician and who leads our student ministry. He takes new students each year and trains them as singers and musicians. This has given us more continuity and a higher level of musical skill. But the day will come when he and his wife complete their studies and return to Ghana and then we will, once again, have to adapt.

JOINT SERVICES

For a number of years we had two or three joint worship services with the French-speaking congregation that owned the building where we met. This was great from the perspective of unity, but I found myself frustrated over time because the goal became to have a service for French and English speakers, not to worship God. The songs we selected were chosen because they could be sung by both congregations, not because they were part of a theme in our worship. In addition, the sermon was translated which made it twice as long. I imagine there are better ways to do this, but I was glad when these services ended.

BALANCE IN LEADERSHIP

When we have had a more Pentecostal style to our worship service, it has been helpful for those in the congregation who were not Pentecostal to have me, an Evangelical, preaching. My style of preaching balanced out the service. On the other hand, several people from Pentecostal backgrounds have mentioned to me over the years that when I arrived, my openness to the Holy Spirit allowed them to feel more welcome.

When someone approaches me who would like to work with me in the church, this balance is always one of my major considerations. We are a congregation of Evangelicals and Pentecostals and there is a benefit to working together in the leadership of the church with men and women from these theological backgrounds. I have worked with Pentecostals and worked with those who have a more conservative theological perspective than mine. The proverb about iron sharpening iron is true and I have benefitted from these relationships. It takes time to learn to work together and trust each other. Initially we drift to the periphery, but eventually we move back to the core and the church benefits as well as us.

MEMBER CARE / COUNSELING

COUNSELING

Expatriates easily understand that they are aliens in a foreign culture. Even those who become fluent in the language know they are not fluent in the culture. This produces stress for expatriates.

David Packer writes in his book that "the international family lives under stress."[28] He then goes on to talk about the work of psychiatrist Thomas H. Holmes who studied the stress of dealing with significant life events and published a scale called "Social Readjustment Rating Scale":

> Researchers have suggested that the accumulation of events within a twelve month period whose points total 200 or more will likely result in some type of long term emotional reaction, ranging from mild depression to anxiety to more serious depression. . . . When people move overseas it is easy to have a personal score of more than 200 points. In fact, I have found that scores of 300 to 400 are not unusual.[29]

One expatriate explained to Packer that "his new assignment was like being sent to a remote spot in the dark, to grasp a large barrel with no handles, and carry it back to the head office without a map. The number of cultural faux pas is seemingly endless."[30]

Packer then asks us to consider:

> The expatriate husband who works all day in an office whose cultural rules he does not understand, coming home to a wife who has had to deal with housekeeping issues that she also does not understand. Just imagine the potential for stress in their marriage and in the home in general. They are also seeking to get their children into a new school, make new friends, find a new church (or perhaps not!), deal with new laws, and, normally, at the same time missing their friends and relatives back home. This is a family filled with people whose continuity quotient in life had just been significantly disrupted.[31]

---

[28] Packer, *Look Who God Let into the Church*, 41.

[29] Packer, 42.

[30] Packer, 44.

[31] Packer, 45.

"The challenges of moving overseas as a single adult can sometimes be even more stressful, for the simple reason that they are separated from their social network."[32]

There are good resources for understanding the stresses of living overseas and I encourage you to read them.[33]

What does a pastor do when members of the community struggle with the stress of living overseas? Because there are so few people trained in counseling in international settings, some people recommend that the pastor needs to develop the skills to counsel and fill the gap. Unfortunately, not all pastors are effective counselors. I have done my best with short-term counseling sessions but I have often regretted that trained counselors were not available. This past year a couple with training in counseling moved to Rabat and this is a huge help. But for fourteen of my fifteen years, this resource was not available. I am excited about their move because of the higher stress that comes with living overseas in a foreign culture. We need the help they bring.

Marriage is not easy in any culture but becomes more difficult because of the stress of living overseas. In *The Meaning of Marriage*, Tim Keller uses the analogy of a ten-ton Mack truck driving across an old bridge:

> There may be hairline fractures that a very close inspection would reveal, but to the naked eye, there is nothing wrong. But now see a ten-ton Mack truck drive onto the bridge. What will happen? The pressure from the weight of the truck will open those hairline fractures so they can be seen. . . . The truck didn't create the weaknesses; it revealed them.[34]

Keller uses this analogy to talk about marriage used by God as a tool of sanctification. Anyone who is married understands the truth of this. But when married couples move overseas, the ten-ton Mack truck takes on additional weight, adding to the stresses of marriage. For this reason, my wife and I have led marriage and parenting courses which have been very well received by couples from a variety of cultures. We use the Relationship Central courses

---

[32] Packer, 45.

[33] Melissa Brayer Hess and Patricia Linderman, *The Expert Expat: Your Guide to Successful Relocation Abroad* (Boston: Nicholas Brealey Publishing, 2007); Robert L. Kohls, *Survival Kit for Overseas Living: For Americans Planning to Live and Work Abroad* (London: Nicholas Brealey Publishing, 2001).

[34] Timothy Keller, *The Meaning of Marriage: Facing the Complexities of Commitment with the Wisdom of God* (New York: Penguin Group, 2011), 139.

taught by Nicky and Sila Lee. These include the *Marriage Course, Parenting Children Course*, and *Parenting Teenagers Course*.[35]

LONG-TERMERS VERSUS SHORT-TERMERS

Each summer and fall as we look eagerly for newcomers, to make them feel welcome and at home in a new community, it is easy to neglect the long-term members of the community. There is so much energy expended getting to know new people, it is easy to take the presence of long-term members for granted.

When people leave our community, we present them with an embroidered banner with the initials of our church. This is made by local believers and is a nice remembrance of their time at RIC. After years of watching people receive these banners, I decided one day to honor the long-term members. At one of our fellowship dinners I held a contest to see who knew the most about Moroccan history and culture and then presented each of them with a banner. This was much appreciated and they felt honored.

David Pederson (Athens, Seoul) points out the need to focus on long-term members:

> Although she never attended our church, Dianne was known and loved by many of the long-term church members. As she was dying of cancer, some members kept asking me to pray for her and, if possible, I should visit her again. When she died, her funeral coincided with a planned outreach event for newcomers that I was personally leading. Since I was not asked to lead the funeral, I decided to divide my time between the events and arrived at the funeral some minutes late. Most in the long-term group were vocal about my absence. It took some years for the event to be forgotten in their minds. Had I given my time completely to the long-term group, the newcomer's outreach may have flopped, but I would have avoided sending the message that "I am not your pastor" to those who saw me as that.[36]

BEING VIEWED AS PASTOR

In an international church with its parade dynamic, it may take time for a pastor to be identified as "my pastor." If there are missionaries in the church, they will have their own groups that meet during the week for prayer and Bible study. The leader of their team is their primary pastor. Others will come from

---

[35] All three of these courses can be found at Relationship Central, http://www.relationshipcentral.org/.

[36] Pederson, *Expatriate Ministry*, 99.

a church where they had a great relationship with their pastor and hold on to that relationship.

God has given me a heart that loves the people in the community I serve as pastor. There are some people who instantly view me as "their pastor" and others who do not. I do not have a problem with those who do not. There are some people who come once a month to our international church and I am pleased to see them each time they come. Whether they feel that I am their pastor or not, I have a calling to be their pastor and love and care for them.

David Pederson (Athens, Seoul) writes that an international pastor knows the difference between the home pastor and the international church pastor:

> Dave and his family had attended our church faithfully for a year since arriving in Athens to work for the embassy. He greeted me after the service one afternoon, "Your messages remind me of my pastor's style of preaching." Before I asked him just who he thought I was, he asked where I had attended seminary and was pleased that it was "his pastor's" seminary.
>
> Becoming "my pastor" takes time. It wasn't until Dave's family was being transferred that he began to call me "my pastor." He also actively worked to get his pastor (me) to accept the vacant post at the church where he and he family moved after Athens.

Pederson adds,

> My pastoral relationship with a transferred short-termer extends for about a year until the short-termer is settled into a new parish. This often involved long-distance counsel and recommendations for new churches to visit."[37]

RAPID INTEGRATION OF GIFTS

The advice given in many churches is to take time with new people before asking them to take responsibility for ministry in the church. International churches do not have that luxury. People arrive in the summer and within a month may be teaching a Sunday School class or leading in worship. Those who have experience and have lived in several countries will come up in the first week and offer their services.

---

[37] Pederson, 97.

Ken MacHarg (Latin America, Europe, Central Asia) gives this illustration:

A key to growth and ministry to expatriates is the ability of international churches (international churches) to rapidly integrate people who start attending into participation and leadership. It is impossible to "wait a year" until a person is totally vetted—by then that person is likely to be gone. Early on we did a two- or three-month exploratory trip to a Latin American country and immediately started to attend an IC. The pastor worked diligently to involve people and within six weeks I had the opportunity to preach several times during our stay. Limiting leadership only to those who are "long-termers" also limits the leadership ability of people who bring gifts and the desire to serve and can provide exciting opportunities to a congregation.

Ray Cobb (Fes) shares a caution:

Great point! Especially the part about not waiting. In our situation in Fes, though, we have found that we do need to wait a while in two areas: leading worship (as opposed to participating in the worship team) and preaching. Too many things get said or done that are not wise from a security issue, and do not take into consideration who we are as a congregation.

Barry Gaeddert (London) comments:

One of the key items in pastoring an international congregation is the fact that you need to quickly move people into leadership positions. This is not the pattern in a typical American church, where you spend time getting to know, training, growing, and developing individuals as leaders. In an international setting they may only be with you for a couple of years, and it is important to capitalize on the leaders that God has sent to you. When I met new people at the start of the year I was always thinking and watching for those that might be good candidates for the leadership roles in our congregation.

My good friend Scott gave me this advice before I went to London. He told me that I needed to think of leadership in terms of campus ministry. The freshman, new to your school, will be the leaders in their junior/senior years. So you will quickly get them involved, go through a short but appropriate training, and then let them lead!

VOLUNTEERS

Churches are always looking for volunteers to help in the church but our experience has been that is more difficult to get volunteers in an international church. Putting an announcement in the bulletin or some other church communication is not very effective in recruiting volunteers. We have discovered that we need to approach people individually in order to find the people needed for the work of the church.

This might be because people come into a new country with a foreign language and culture and need time to adjust. The church is not like the church they have been used to and so they are a bit more reluctant to stick their neck out and volunteer.

Ray Cobb (Fes) comments:

> Part of flexibility can also be willing to say, "sorry," no one has felt led to step forward to help with ... whatever. We will not be having this "...." at this time. We have had to do this a number of times—sometimes it is a small issue—refreshments after the service. No one has signed up for clean-up so no refreshments. The solution is not to see the person who already does so much do this yet again. Once we had to decrease the age at which Sunday School would be offered from 11 to 9 years of age. There were just not those willing to teach, and it has actually worked out quite well.

LOOSE CANNONS

There are Christian workers who pass through highly transitional international churches who have no affiliation. Without an organization behind them, they are independent and I am always cautious with people like this until I get to know them better. There was one woman who had some emotional issues and her wealthy family supported her in Morocco. She created problems in the Moroccan churches with inappropriate relationships. She was unpredictable and we were never sure what she would say or do. If she had belonged to an organization we could have talked to the leadership but in her case, there was no one to talk to. Her family seemed happy to have her an ocean away.

Some years before we arrived in Rabat, friends of ours who lived in a North African country were attending a conference and an itinerant evangelist from the West was taking care of their ten-year old son and another young man. He sodomized both of them at knifepoint and threatened to kill their parents if they said anything to anyone. It did not come out for a few more years until the boys came into puberty and began acting out. Interpol sought after this man, but justice is illusive in this world.

This story was in my head when I arrived and so I have always kept my antennae up when people pass through. One Sunday a young man arrived, traveling by himself with no organizational affiliation. He expressed interest in working with the church. When I talked with him afterward at the Adult Sunday School class, I noticed he had traces of mascara on his eyelids. His behavior and mannerisms seemed a bit strange.

After church I sent an email to all the other international pastors in Morocco, telling them his name, nationality, and a brief description. I said I had no evidence of any wrongdoing, but I urged caution if he came and said I would not want him to be alone with any of the children in the church. International churches welcome people in so frequently that it is important that any red flags are shared with each other.

FELLOWSHIP

In a diverse congregation with no other alternatives, we do not limit our friendships to those who are like us because there are not very many people like us. So we cross over racial, denominational, national, educational, and economic lines in the relationships we build.

Visitors to our church admire the way we relate across these lines. I have noticed that this is especially true of those who come from mainline denominations where the trinity of Father, Son, and Holy Spirit seems to have been replaced by the trinity of Diversity, Tolerance, and Inclusion.

My contention, and the experience in our church here in Rabat, is that when we focus on the Triune God: Father, Son, and Holy Spirit, we become more inclusive and more diverse. "God so loved the world," John wrote in his Gospel. Because God loves the world and not just any one particular part of the world, when we focus on him, lift praise to him in worship, and try to become more like Christ, our hearts will be opened to all the world, not just the part most like us.

TENSIONS

We have wonderfully diverse friendships at RIC but that does not mean we are without relational tensions. Some of these come from cultural misunderstandings.

A young, single American came to work in the U.S. Embassy on his first overseas assignment. He befriended one of the Nigerians who came into the country to try to play football with a club and whose legal status in the country was questionable. They met together and the American invited this man to go with him and some other friends for a weekend trip. The Nigerian kept talking about buying groceries and cooking for themselves because he knew even that would be a stretch for his budget. But when they got there, they all went out to eat at restaurants where his share of the meals amounted to three or four weeks of what he normally spent on food. He did not have money with him for this but was embarrassed and said he would pay his share when he returned. He came to see me when he returned to Rabat to talk about this. He had money saved for a ticket out of Morocco to pursue playing for another club and had to use this money to repay the debt of the weekend. I ended up helping him repay the money and then explained to the American the reality of life for a migrant. I did not want to discourage the relationship, but both of them had to be more aware and more honest about their different economic situations.

Another part of this tension was that in African culture, when you invite someone to come with you, it is expected that you will pay for the person you invite. But in American culture, each person is expected to pay their own share.

When we have a Seder meal during Easter week, to cover the cost of the food we charge seventy-five dirhams (a bit less than ten USD) per person with discounts for families. This automatically makes the meal inaccessible to a significant part of the congregation. So what should we do? We could subsidize the cost of the meal for all those who cannot afford it. We could cancel the meal, but that deprives those who are able to pay of the meaningful experience. (Every year there are a few people who pay extra so others can participate.)

What I have learned over the years is that when we try to create programs for the whole of the church, they are not quite successful. We do much better when we create programs for the different segments of the church and then come together to worship on Sunday.

As an example, we have a men's Bible study that currently meets for lunch on Wednesdays. This study is not announced in the church bulletin or RICEmail. It is open by invitation only and is reserved for diplomats and businessmen. If it was opened up to anyone, the diplomats and businessmen would be less likely to meet. So in order to preserve this time for this part of the church community, it is done without being announced in church.

We do the same with the Alpha Course. The course starts with a meal and then after watching the DVD presentation, there is dessert with small group discussion. People in the small groups take turns providing the food we eat. If

I opened this up to the whole church, we could be inundated with people who are not from a culture that brings food to events like this and the tone of the evening would be completely different. The people we would like to come would be less likely to come. So we limited the Alpha Course to our target audience and then later had a student Alpha Course for which RIC provided sandwiches. This has worked much better.

David and Daphne Fisher (Lisbon, Madrid) give this illustration of tension due to cultural misunderstanding:

> About a year ago, a single man in our community lost his mother in the States to suicide. It was a tremendous struggle for him that he did not have the funds to buy his ticket. Pete (a pseudonym) asked us if the church could help and so the church gave Pete the funds to buy his ticket. But, when he waited more than a week to leave, a Portuguese team member became very upset and decided that Pete had tricked us out of the money. In Portugal, he explained to us, he would NEVER go visit family AFTER the funeral. It was critical to attend the funeral and as funerals happen within one or two days of the death, Pete obviously had no intention to go. You would never go a week or two later to visit your relative just to see if they were okay.
>
> That last statement shocked us Americans at how uncaring it sounded—that you wouldn't visit the widow or family to show ongoing love! And, although we explained to our team member that in the USA it's not uncommon to delay a funeral service—or merely have a memorial service, he remained unconvinced. (In fact, Pete's mother's death is still being investigated and the memorial service was held three months after her death.)

LANGUAGE BARRIERS

I have talked about language difficulties earlier but haven't mentioned that language barriers prevent us from developing deeper friendships. When we can't easily converse, it is difficult to get to know people on a deeper level. I have suggested we measure our language fluency by our IQ in each language we speak. If I walk into a hardware store where English is spoken, I will say, "I am looking for a small, brass clamp to restrict the flow of water on the hose of my water filter." If I have to ask in French, I will say, "I am looking for something to make less water go through a hose." If I ask in Arabic, I will say, "I want a little water."

These language barriers can cause tension in the fellowship of an international church. Once I had to intervene between two women, both of whom spoke English as a third language. They each assumed they had communicated but each had misunderstood the other.

I sit in meetings when French is being spoken and have learned that if the topic is sensitive, I have to ask for translation because I am missing the nuances of what is being said. I realize also that when I speak English, even if the other person is nodding, what I am saying is not always being understood. One June I told our gardener (a Moroccan who speaks a bit of French) that I wanted to trim back our bougainvillea in the fall. He said, "D'accord," meaning, "Yes, I agree with you," and the next week he had trimmed it back, cutting away all the beautiful flowers we had been enjoying.

Stephen Rhodes gives this illustration: (While he is not pastor of an international church, his experience comes from being pastor of a multiethnic church in the US.)

> When I first came to Culmore, one of the biggest problems we had to overcome in order to be one congregation was the barrier of understanding and being understood. Even though the church had been ethnically diverse for many years, there was still little communication among the members. Recent Filipino immigrants kept company with other Filipinos; the same was true with Latinos, Anglos and others.
>
> One day I was having a conversation with an older Anglo member, who brought up this fact. I asked her why she thought this was the case. She said that she could speak only for herself: she was simply afraid of being embarrassed at not understanding what was being said to her. In speaking with several of the immigrant members of Culmore, she had found herself either asking for repetition or simply smiling and nodding her head in acknowledgment—without having the slightest idea what the person was saying.[38]

David Packer gives this illustration of tension due to language problems in talking about a major conflict in the international church in Singapore:

---

[38] Stephen Rhodes, *Where the Nations Meet: The Church in a Multicultural World* (Downers Grove, IL: IVP, 1998), 69.

In looking back over the things that were written and being said at the time, I realized that unfortunately, many times our communication in meetings was not understood by all, even though all were speaking English. Sometimes accents and speed of talk made it difficult if not completely impossible for all in the room to understand what was being said.[39]

I have regrets that my lack of language skills has prevented me from knowing some people more deeply. This creates tensions because it can seem that I do not want to know a person better and that person might feel slighted. The facility with which someone speaks English can also prevent me from knowing the depth of a person.

Stephen Rhodes gives this illustration about Tomas, a man from Nicaragua who was a professor in Managua and now worked two manual-labor jobs. Tomas was a student in an ESL class Rich taught.

Rich thought he was beginning to get to know Tomas fairly well, but he realized how little he really knew him when, one night, a bilingual Culmore member joined them in conversation. She was able to translate not only Tomas's words but also the depth of his feeling and character. Rich said that the Tomas who was revealed in that conversation was a deeply thoughtful and intellectual man with a poetic and compassionate soul. Until that moment, Rich said, he had caught only glimpses of who Tomas really was. With the aid of a translator, he was able to experience Tomas the professor instead of Tomas the student.[40]

FAVORITISM

In a diverse congregation where we gear the programs to the different parts of the church, we open ourselves to the charge of favoritism. When I am aware there is an issue such as this, my approach is to address it head on. So in my preaching from James, when I came to James 2:1–7 that deals with favoritism, I talked about what people were thinking but not saying:

My brothers, show no partiality as you hold the faith in our Lord Jesus Christ, the Lord of glory. For if a man wearing a gold ring and fine clothing comes into your assembly, and a poor man in shabby

---

[39]   Packer, *Look Who God Let into the Church*, 138.

[40]   Rhodes, 72.

clothing also comes in, and if you pay attention to the one who wears
the fine clothing and say, "You sit here in a good place," while you say
to the poor man, "You stand over there," or, "Sit down at my feet," have
you not then made distinctions among yourselves and become judges
with evil thoughts?

I asked,

> Do you think we show favoritism here at RIC? Do we pay more
> attention to some people than others? Is everyone welcome here or are
> some people more welcome than others? Do we pay more attention to
> white Americans and Europeans than we do to black Africans? Do we
> pay more attention to those who can afford to give more to the church
> than we do to those who have limited financial resources?

When I said this there was almost an audible gasp, and then I gave some
examples of behavior at RIC that is not favoritism:

> Seeking out people who are like you is not favoritism. If you are
> sitting in your chair on Sunday when new people are welcomed and
> you hear someone say they are from your country, it is natural that
> you would want to meet them and find out specifically which city they
> came from. When you come to RIC, it is natural that you make friends
> and hang out with people who come from your country or who share
> much of your culture.

> When someone comes from the U.S. I am curious to know what
> part of the U.S. they come from and if we, perhaps, know some people
> in common. When someone comes to the church who is approximately
> my age, I am interested in talking with them. It is natural to want to
> meet people who share my nationality, my culture, and my age.

I used the example of young men and women in their twenties who
come to RIC and prefer going to a café after church with people their own age
rather than coming with me to the Adult Sunday School which is composed of
those who are, for the most part, people twice their age. They are not showing
favoritism; they are simply moving to their comfort zone. We are comfortable
seeking out those who are like us, who understand us. This is normal. This is
natural. This is not favoritism.

I went on to say that while it is natural to seek your comfort zone, if you
come to RIC with its more than thirty-five nationalities and more than forty

denominations and do not make an effort to establish friendships with people from other countries and backgrounds, you are missing out on one of the great blessings of this church.

Among all the people who have blessed me, one in particular stands out. A man from the southern tip of India came to our home for a meal. We sat down at a table with silverware and plates and after I said grace, he excused himself, got up, and went to the bathroom to wash his hands. When he came back he began to eat with his fingers. He had never before used silverware and told me that from where he came, they would put a banana leaf on the ground, put the food on that, and then share the meal. The next time he came to our house we did not put out our silverware and we all ate with our fingers.

This man had a deep faith and trust in Jesus and I learned a lot from watching him trust Jesus in difficult circumstances. I prayed with him for his wife and son who were being threatened by other members of the family. He was unable to fly home to help them and all he could do was to pray and trust God to help them. That is what happened. The family issue was resolved and I learned that my wealth that allows me to fly home and fix problems deprives me of growing in faith as I trust in God to make things work out. My life is richer because of my friendship with this man.

These cross-cultural relationships have enriched my life and understanding and I want those who come to our church to have the same blessing I have had.

POTLUCKS—"BRING & SHARE"

For more than fifty years RIC depended on the generosity of another church who allowed us to use their facility. But in 2013 we took a step of faith and began to rent our own facility. I mention this because for almost all of my time at RIC we were not able to share meals together at the church and went to the home of someone in the church for our potluck meals. But once we moved into our new villa and decided to have a potluck, a minor issue with potlucks became a major issue.

African culture is not a potluck culture. In African churches people will make food and carry it for a family gathering, but not to a church meal. They will bring food to give to the pastor, but not to be shared in church. When we moved from the church to one of our homes for a potluck meal, there was always sufficient attrition in the move to the home so that there were more people who brought food and less who came without food. But when we had our potluck meal after our service at the church there was no attrition and more than half of the people had not brought any food to share. Even though many of us had brought extra food, by the time the end of the line came to get something, nothing was left.

As a consequence, we decided that if we will have a traditional potluck, we will continue to hold it in the home of someone in the church. When we have a potluck at the church we will simplify the menu and serve soup and sandwiches, or provide most of the meal.

In addition, "potluck" is an American term not understood by the rest of the world. Hot dish is another unknown term. One woman asked how many chilies she should put in her hot dish, four or eight? We have begun to call "potlucks" "Bring & Shares" because that communicates better what happens at the meal.

There was also a problem with people taking too much food so there was little or nothing left at the end of the line. I am not sure of all the reasons why this is. Perhaps those with less money in the church do not have the opportunity to eat food like this and so overindulge. Or perhaps it is a cultural style. I have observed that when the African students have a group meal, there are servers who regulate how much is put on the plates. I saw the same at a potluck with Gibraltarians. So we plan in the future to have people serve those who come through the line. This indicates a lack of trust to Westerners, but we all have to adapt to the cultures around us.

SOCIAL MEDIA

If you do a web search for "church in Rabat," the RIC website is usually the first that comes up. So I often get emails from people intending to move to Rabat and wanting to know more about the church. Some of them follow the weekly sermon posts to get a flavor of my preaching before they arrive. I ask them if they would like to be put on our weekly RICEmail and they always say yes. (Our weekly email is called RICEmail.) After receiving our RICEmails for a few months, when they arrive they feel a bit less like strangers and are able to fit in to our community more easily.

David Pederson, in his book *Expatriate Ministry: Inside the Church of the Outsiders*, identifies numerous challenges that are unique to an international church. One of these challenges is a lack of visibility. RIC meets in a building that has no sign to indicate a church meets in that villa. Everyone in the neighborhood knows a church meets there, but in the public/private culture of Morocco, it is less offensive to the neighbors to meet without a banner proclaiming a church meets in the neighborhood. People have to know where we meet because they will not find us by walking down the street.

This is not the case for international churches that meet in established church buildings. For the first ten years I was here, we met in a church built by the French in downtown Rabat. People walking by would see that it was a church. But in either case, our website has been very important to helping people know about our existence and helping people find us.

Ken MacHarg (Latin America, Europe, Central Asia) comments:

Churches, especially in restricted countries, may not be able to advertise or put up a sign. They must find other ways to be intentional about letting people know they are around. I have met people in churches who will tell me they had been in the country for five or six years but had just become aware of the existence of an international church.

More and more people find an international church in a particular city through a web search for a website or a Facebook page. Most visitors to ICP (Prague) tell me that they found us through our website. A pastor of a Baptist international church in Germany told a conference last year that his new church plant grew 45 percent in one month primarily through targeted advertising on their Facebook page. It is primarily a student church in a university community.

CHURCH HOME

As I mentioned, for the first thirteen years of my time here at RIC and for all the previous years RIC has existed, RIC met in a church owned or rented by someone else. This was always a struggle. For the first ten years I was pastor, we were sandwiched between a Korean service and a French service. When the Korean service went too long, we had little or no time to set up for our service and then had to shorten our service so we would finish on time. This happened far too frequently and sometimes we did not shorten the service and moved past our ending time which irritated the leaders of the French service that followed. When we wanted to use the church for a special Easter or Christmas service, we had to ask permission and then take whatever time was given to us.

The most difficult part of these years was that we did not have a church home. There was no place where people could come during the week for meetings or just to meet and talk. All of our meetings were held in different homes. We very much appreciated the generosity of the churches that allowed us to share their facility, and they were gracious to us, but we did not have the flexibility of having our own space and did not have a sense of home where we belonged.

Now that we have our own building we are discovering the benefits and challenges of having our own space. We have more responsibility now that the maintenance and regulation of the villa is on our shoulders, but having our own home has given us a sense of security. Our church villa is a haven in which we can rest.

PRAYER

CULTURAL

It is helpful to realize that our forms of prayer are cultural. When I first became a follower of Jesus, to pray out loud was a terrifying prospect and the first several times I did this I was nervous, red in the face, sweating. But over time I learned from others what to say and how to say it. After years of praying in small groups and perhaps in church, it seems second nature to us and we do not realize how cultural our prayers are. But when you come to an international church, this becomes more obvious.

For a brief time I went to an early morning Korean prayer service. It met five mornings a week, at 5 a.m. I went just on Thursday mornings. When they prayed, it sounded as if the roof was going to lift off. Loud, shouting prayers, deafening. It was impossible for me to pray myself and so I sat and listened as they shouted out their prayers.

Many of the African prayers follow a pattern that begins softly with many insertions of Scripture, "As it says in 2 Chronicles 7:14...." The volume and intensity slowly builds to a crescendo of "breaking the power of Satan" and "in Jesus' name" and then slowly dies down to a conclusion. This takes five or more minutes. I mentioned already that all-night prayer meetings are part of African culture. The night is when evil lurks and so that is the best time to do spiritual warfare.

There have been others who come to pray in Morocco and believe that there are spiritual power lines between the minarets of mosques. So they stand in the middle and break the power of Islam. Some have told me that people speak curses onto cassette tapes (this was a few years ago when cassette tapes were still being used) and then spool out the tape on the street as a way of spreading the curse to all who pass by.

There are a lot of very strange things that are believed and prayed for. I would not be comfortable with these prayers at a church meeting, but in a private home, unless I see a grave danger, I do not interfere.

I have learned to adapt to other cultural patterns of prayer and what I look for is not a certain style, but authenticity.

After a Sunday morning worship service at RIC, some students (from African countries) discerned that a woman was possessed by demons. They brought her upstairs to the prayer room and proceeded to pray for deliverance. The door was closed, but the prayers were still loud and two men from the Western world heard what was happening and were uncomfortable with the loud prayers.

When the cultures of the world come together our cultural patterns of prayer will clash. In this case it was two men from a Baptist background disturbed by the prayers of students from Pentecostal churches. I was away when this happened and needed to speak to the two men and hear their perspective and then help them to see that while these prayers were different, they were not wrong.

David Packer (Singapore, Stuttgart) gives this illustration:

> One missionary guest house I visited in Manila had in their list of rules for their guests, "No praying after 10:00 p.m." I asked what they meant by that and they said, "Well, that is for our Korean guests." They had often been visited by Korean church groups on mission trips, and most of the groups, she said, "whenever they prayed, they all prayed passionately, loud and long. The tightness of Korean culture tended to re-affirm that this was the right way for Christians to pray. The guest house was located in a neighborhood and the loud praying of Korean Christians had disturbed the neighbors, hence the need for the house rule. Then the manager told me, "You are Americans. You can pray after 10:00 p.m."[41]

PRAYING IN ANOTHER LANGUAGE

When a Christian group comes from the U.S. to experience Morocco for a week, meeting with Moroccan followers of Jesus is always a delight and often they want a person to pray for them in Arabic. The same has been true when one of my Moroccan friends traveled to the U.S. with me and we visited different churches. And there is something wonderful about this, that people from different lands and speaking different languages are my brothers and sisters in Christ. Despite our communication difficulties, we are one family.

---

[41] Packer, *Look Who God Let into the Church*, 109.

We often have meetings during which people will pray in their own language. This is a good thing, but if I happen not to speak that language, then I sit, not comprehending, trusting that good things are being prayed for.

It was during one of those times when I could not understand a long prayer being prayed that I thought about Paul's rebuke of the church in Corinth:

> What then shall we say, brothers? When you come together, everyone has a hymn, or a word of instruction, a revelation, a tongue or an interpretation. All of these must be done for the strengthening of the church. If anyone speaks in a tongue, two—or at the most three—should speak, one at a time, and someone must interpret. If there is no interpreter, the speaker should keep quiet in the church and speak to himself and God.[42]

Paul wanted there to be order in the meetings of the church and speaking in tongues, which was unintelligible to others, without anyone to interpret what was being said, was disorderly. So what would Paul say about a service where people pray in their native language which most other people do not understand? I think he would ask, "In what way does this edify the church?"

I have a Moroccan friend who made the journey from Islam to Jesus in part because he did not understand why Allah could speak only Arabic. In contrast, he went to a wedding of two Moroccan Christians with many foreigners present and when everyone prayed for the couple in their own language, he viewed this as confirmation of the choice he had made to follow Jesus because God could understand all the languages of the world. So even though it can be an encouragement, I think it wise and helpful to have translation of prayers as much as possible.

CHURCH GOVERNANCE

RIC has a constitution and by-laws that we periodically revise to bring them into conformity with the changing nature of the church. These call for two Semi-Annual General Meetings (SAGM) per year at which we conduct the official business of the church. We receive reports, approve a budget, elect new board members, and make whatever specific decisions that arise.

What makes a good pastor or church board member in a home country does not necessarily make a good pastor or board member in an international church. Vision is highly praised as a leadership skill but it is not as necessary in

---

[42] 1 Corinthians 14:26-28.

an international church. In most international churches we have a vague past and a limited future. A five-year plan does not mean much to someone who comes in year two and leaves in year four.

We pastor a parade and this means that relationships are far more important than vision and organization. The responsibility of pastor and board member is to build and encourage others to build relationships that will nurture us in the few short years we are together in an international church.

KEEP IT SIMPLE—MAKE IT FLEXIBLE

The pastor who preceded me did a wonderful job developing our constitution and by-laws. But we have had to make some changes over the years because we found ourselves in the position of violating our by-laws because we were not able to comply. For example, our by-laws said that one member of the board is supposed to recruit two or more people from the congregation to form a nominating committee to nominate new board members. The selections need to be announced at least two weeks before a SAGM. This is a good policy, but the reality was that we weren't able to do this. Sometimes we have been able to announce the nominations two weeks before the meeting, but often, because of the transitional nature of our church, the process has been much more informal. The new by-laws have simplified the process and bring us into conformity with our general practice.

There will be board members who are process-oriented and will want strict adherence to the constitution and by-laws. Others will be willing to be flexible when the situation demands it. So when creating or revising the constitution and by-laws to reflect the changing nature of the church, it is best to build in some flexibility so when deviation from the norm is helpful, the constitution and by-laws are still being adhered to. The simpler the by-laws are, the more an international church will be able to abide by them. Rather than create a by-law for every contingency, it is better to deal with issues as they arrive.

SELECTION OF BOARD MEMBERS

We try to have a board that represents a wide range of people in the congregation. When we make decisions, we want to be sensitive to how the various cultures of the church view a certain issue. We have benefitted enormously by having a diverse board. We try to have male and female representation. Since half of our congregation is from sub-Saharan Africa, it is important to have African representation. We need board members who can help us interpret cultural behaviors and expectations.

For example, when we moved into our new villa, we had to deal with whether or not people would be permitted to sleep in the villa overnight. Could the university students hold a retreat and have eighty to a hundred people sleeping and taking showers in the villa for a week? In our discussion it became clear that there was a Western view and an African view of how a church should be used. Africans are accustomed to the church being used as a place to sleep in special situations. Westerners have other options and would help those people find a hotel. So it was critical that we had a couple Africans on the board who could help us understand the expectation of the students.

It is also important that those who serve on the board are sympathetic to those in the church who have come to Morocco because they want people in this country to hear the good news that they are loved by Jesus. When board members are opposed to this, then the board is not able to discuss all that needs to be discussed. For this reason, it is best for the pastor and board to vet the names that are nominated before they are brought to the congregation.

PASTOR'S ROLE AS A LEADER

In a church where the board can change significantly every six months, there is a need for stability. This means that a pastor of an international church will need to take a stronger role in leadership. David Packer speaks to this:

> Due to the multi-cultural nature and the turnover in the congregation, an international church's leadership teeters on a very narrow balancing beam. At any time it may tip one way or the other due to shifts in the ethnic percentages of the church membership. Ethnicity was not the only issue, as often people from the same ethnic group have different opinions. New people bring new ideas. As a pastor I felt that part of my job was to try to keep us on a somewhat even keel, in a somewhat steady direction. I had to balance letting the current crop of expatriated leaders have some influence, with avoiding wild swings in varying directions.[43]

EXPECTATIONS BASED ON PREVIOUS
CHURCH EXPERIENCE

One of the challenges for the pastor arises when a board member wants the church to function the way it did in a previous church he or she attended. In one particular example, a board member came from an international church

---

[43]   Packer, *Look Who God Let into the Church*, 50.

that had a high percentage of local believers. This made the church much less transitional. In discussions of what we should do as a church, the programs this man wanted to introduce would not work in our highly transitional community. But because they had worked in his previous international church, he assumed they would work in our international church.

Another man who worked with me as an associate pastor wanted to introduce a series of teaching opportunities. Over the course of three years we would cover the Bible, basic theology, and Christian living. It was a great set of courses, but much too comprehensive for what we are able to handle. It took this man about a year before he realized that this schedule was just not going to work in our highly transitional church. What works best is having short courses, not more than seven weeks long.

It is important to continually remind board members about the distinct dynamics of our international church.

David Pederson (Athens, Seoul) comments:

> All people seem to bring their pet projects into the church thinking that it will work as well as it did at home, but it is not always the case in an international church. You have to be much more flexible.[44]

Mark DeYmaz comments:

> Church leaders who are inflexible, or unwilling to think outside the box, will struggle with the frequent tension that is inevitable when leading a multi-ethnic church. Some may seek to spiritualize issues to mask their own insecurities or agenda, or they will want to narrowly define everything from the style of worship to the strategy for evangelism. More often than not, while these leaders are arguing for the "biblical" approach, their opinions will be rooted in their own personalities, past experiences, or cultural perspectives, to the exclusion of others who differ from them. Such people must not be allowed to control the direction of the whole.[45]

John Carlock (Cairo) gives a story about a pastor starting a second service:

> The pastor before me had been here at HCC for about a year. The church at the time was growing and about 70–80 percent full

---

[44] Pederson, *Expatriate Ministry*, 54.
[45] Mark DeYmaz & Harry Li, *Ethnic Blends*, 163.

on Friday morning and he had decided he would go ahead and start a second Friday morning service. He did this without consulting the leadership team or seeking much input from other people in the church. It caused a lot of problems because there was a feeling that our Friday morning service was the only time our community came together. He had not considered how important community was to the church. The first service ended, there was fellowship, and then the second service would start a half hour later. But still it wasn't the same as the community worshiping together and then spending time in fellowship afterwards. The pastor used a concept we use in the United States. If the service is 70 percent full it is time to build or to start a second service. He carried that over to the church here in Cairo and it caused a lot of problems. This is one example of how an international church is different from a church in the United States.

CONTINUITY

I came to Rabat in September 1999 to visit RIC and explore the possibility that I would come as pastor. I met several times with the eight or nine people on the church board, and when I arrived three months later to begin as pastor of RIC, more than half of the board was no longer living in Rabat. (I told those who left that theirs was a cheap decision because they did not have to live with the consequences of their choice.) An international church is a transitional church and the leadership of the church moves along with the rest of the congregation.

This high rate of transition makes continuity very important. The by-laws of RIC try to deal with this by electing board members to one-year terms with half of the board (ideally) elected at each of the two Semi-Annual General Meetings. This means that at least half of the board has some knowledge of what has been happening in recent months. When people serve multiple terms, the board has more continuity that is very helpful.

This is not an easy situation for a pastor since the board character can change so often and so suddenly. There have been boards that did not want to be too involved in the church, and as pastor, I made the adjustment to taking on more of the responsibility. When a new board was elected that wanted to be very involved in the decision making of the church, I was slow to react and there were some tensions until I readjusted my expectations. An international pastor needs to assess the new board and be ready to make quick adjustments.

With the high rate of transition, it is very helpful when the pastor serves for a longer period of time. The pastor can help the board remember past decisions so the board does not continually cycle through the same issue over and over again. If the dynamics in the church have changed, perhaps the issue needs to be revisited, but most often this is not the case.

One example of this is RIC's position on illegal migration. After a long discussion we decided that while illegal migrants are welcome in our church, they are not permitted to lead by singing in the choir, ushering, or serving in any other official way. We had good reasons for formulating this policy and the new boards do not need to reconsider this position every couple years.

David Packer (Singapore, Stuttgart) comments:

> In any church it is difficult to get closure on some issues—even more so in an international church. You can elect a committee to do a study of some issue, the committee can take several months to examine the matter, and then they can report back to the church body with their findings and the church can then make a decision, but then the very next week a new family can come into the church and ask if you had ever thought about doing the very opposite thing from the decision you just made! Of course, they are quite innocent in the matter. They had no idea what the church had just been through.[46]

RECORD HISTORY OF CONFLICTS AND OTHER MAJOR DECISIONS

When there is a conflict in the church with someone, it is helpful to write down a history of that conflict, complete with the actions of the board that were taken. It might be several years later and a couple of generations of church membership and board members before the situation arises again, and the new board will need an orientation to the history of the relationship between the church and that person. If there is a new pastor, this record will help sort out the variations of memories about what happened.

MEMBERSHIP

When I arrived at RIC there were no official members, just a process that determined who was able to vote at one of the two semi-annual meetings. There were by-laws that tried to protect the church from being taken over by a block of fifteen or twenty people who could come to a Semi-Annual General Meeting and control the decisions being made. This seemed unnecessarily complicated and after a year or so, we modified the by-laws by adding a category of membership.

---

[46]   Packer, *Look Who God Let into the Church*, 50.

This was not done when the by-laws were first written, I suspect, because this is a highly transitional church. But borrowing from my PCUSA background, we began having "Affiliate Members." This category of membership is used in the PCUSA for people who come to a community for a short time, university students, for example, and do not want to give up membership in their home church.

This worked well but eventually people began asking me how they could become "real" members and I realized that because denominations are losing their influence, affiliate membership was no longer meeting a need. So we dropped "affiliate" and have just "members" now.

I tell people that in this age of temporary relationships, it is important for Christians to make commitments with each other and that it is an important part of their spiritual life to commit to RIC for the time they are with us.

NECESSARY INFORMALITY

Except for much larger international churches, policies and procedures are often necessarily informal. This story from David Pederson points out the informality of the candidating process as well as the theological diversity of an international church:

> The church could not afford to have us come to Athens for a look-see, so they sent a trusted long-term member and his wife who met us at O'Hare airport for an interview. We ducked into a bar and sat on stools around a small, round table. Len's eyes were warm and steady. Lorraine was full of adventure. Each of them ordered a large stein of beer. Then Len leaned over and asked me what I thought about infant baptism. We were a young teetotaling Free Church couple. They were older Lutherans who loved the Lord too. We fell in love with the diversity of the international congregation from that moment on. We committed to accept the call on the spot. The only roadblock was the health of our firstborn, due in six weeks. When Hilary arrived healthy and strong, we bought our tickets and arrived in Athens seven weeks later.[47]

FINANCES

RECORD KEEPING

When I arrived as pastor, I began reading through the files in the church office and one thing I noticed was the high turnover in church treasurers. In

---

[47]   Pederson, *Expatriate Ministry*, 108.

one of the recent years before I arrived, there had been five church treasurers in one year. What this meant is that the church finances were not kept in good order. This was a problem when we were using the facility of another church and had fewer bills to pay. But now that we are in our own facility, it has become even more critical to keep consistent financial records.

Given my business background, when I arrived and assessed the situation, I realized this was one way I could serve the church and I assumed the responsibility for record keeping. I am fully aware of the discussion of having the pastor focus on spiritual issues without knowing how much members are contributing, but the need for consistency overruled those concerns.

Obviously, if the pastor is keeping the financial records, the big need is for accountability and so the board member serving as church treasurer, along with one other person, counts the offering each Sunday and fills out a slip with all the details. Then, each month—ideally—the treasurer meets with me to go over the record keeping to make sure everything was entered properly.

With our move into our own facility, our budget has increased dramatically and the financial responsibility has also increased. It takes more and more time to keep the financial records in order but I am working on a system that will be less dependent on me.

The key is continuity and if there is a long-term member of the church who is good with finances and willing to serve as a long-term treasurer, that is the best solution. The need for consistency is also important because it is often difficult for an international church to get a bank account. Currently, there are two people in RIC who are able to sign checks and two signatures are required for each check. If either of the two people is away, we cannot write checks. But to make a change requires taking our official statutes and supporting documents to the bank which is not an easy process. We will be adding three more people to the check signing authorization and the longevity of those people is a prime consideration.

BENEFIT OF A PASTOR RAISING SUPPORT

The demographics of our church make it a challenge to raise the funds needed for our budget. Half of our congregation is students receiving a scholarship from UNESCO. They are supposed to receive another scholarship from their home countries, but because of political instability and corruption in their countries, they sometimes do not receive this. There are women married to Moroccans whose husbands control the family finances and do not want them giving to the church. There are some who come to Morocco as missionaries and they have limited incomes. There are diplomats and military officers who come but they are here for a limited period of time and may not feel invested in the church until a good portion of their time has passed. Others come but feel led, and sometimes are obligated, to continue supporting their home church.

This means that an international church will probably not be in a position to pay a pastoral salary. They may be able to help with ministry expenses, but most often a pastor will have to find his or her own support.

For my first ten years, I provided my own support out of funds I had from the sale of a business. But then, five years ago, because of the decline in the value of the dollar and the drop in the stock market, I was depleting savings necessary for retirement and had to begin raising support.

To my surprise, I discovered this to be a highly beneficial activity. It has given me opportunities to share what is happening in Morocco and raise the number of people who pray for me. (I had always viewed prayer letters asking for support as letters looking for funds with prayer just an add-on. But when I arrived in Morocco I discovered the importance of people praying for me and I am amazed and delighted when I visit a church and someone comes up to me to tell me they pray for me every week. I am humbled by this gift of support.)

So I encourage even those who are able to supply their own funds to raise support for their work in an international church. You can give more yourself if you wish, but the benefits of raising support are important.

FAITH GROWING

Financial pledges do not work in such a transitional community. We have had years of plenty and years of famine. I am not uncomfortable preaching about financial stewardship. How we use our money and possessions is an important part of our spiritual life. But I choose not to manipulate giving with messages about giving. I strongly believe that money follows the heart. So I preach the love of God. I preach Christ and his work for us. I preach the work of the Holy Spirit to transform us and how this gives us hope.

We have paid our bills every year. Sometimes we have used up almost all of our reserves, other years we have been able to have a surplus. But I have learned not to worry and trust for what we need. Budgets come and go but the faith God grows as we trust in him will last for eternity.

When we began to think about finding our own facility, I was very overwhelmed. Year by year, we had barely met our budget. In the first two years I was here, two families tithed and provided 75 percent of our budget. But then they left and we began rapidly using up our surplus funds. In the following years we would meet at the SAGM in May, halfway through our fiscal year, and talk about how we could cut our budget. It was often a huge challenge and some years we used up our reserves. We never ended a year in debt, but we entered into some years with no financial cushion. So to contemplate increasing our budget by 175 percent in order to move into our own facility was quite daunting.

We met for a day of fasting and prayer in September 2012 and although we did not have a clear sense of direction at the end of the day, within two weeks it was clear to us that we should look for a villa we could rent.

At our SAGM that November, those present were positive about taking on this new responsibility. We found a villa and signed a contract at the end of December. Then we began raising funds for our setup costs: audio, video, chairs, etc. The amount we needed to raise was more than our previous year's budget, but by April we had raised those funds and began meeting in our new facility in May. We finished the 2013/2014 fiscal year in the black and since then have been able to maintain the level of giving to meet our increased expenses. When you add to the increased budget the setup funds we raised, this is quite amazing.

The reason I am sharing this is to encourage others in international churches to not be fearful when you sense God leading you to take a step of faith. Despite the years of struggling to meet our budget, when we stepped out to where we believe God led us, purses were opened and we have been blessed.

WEDDINGS AND FUNERALS

Weddings and funerals are not a significant part of ministry at RIC. In fifteen years I have officiated at just seven funerals for people who attended RIC and three or four for expatriates who were not from the church community. I have officiated at just four weddings.

FUNERALS

I often feel uncomfortable officiating at a funeral for someone from a culture different than mine. I think, especially at funerals, there is a need for the cultural forms that help to deal with the death of a loved one. I do the best I can, but would love to have a resource that would help me to know the cultural forms for the countries of the world so I could adapt what I say and do to that culture.

WEDDINGS

Because we are a transitional community, when people meet and decide to get married they tend to go back to their family and home community for the marriage. Although weddings are not a large part of ministry in this international church, there are some issues.

There is a romantic feel to a Moroccan wedding and so periodically I am contacted to see if I will officiate for a couple wanting to get married. They want to fly into Morocco, get married, and spend a week here before flying home. I require five pre-marital counseling sessions before I will officiate at a wedding and while it is possible that a pastor in their community could do this counseling and I could accept that, this has never happened. Most people wanting to come to Morocco for a wedding do not have much of a church background.

The easiest way for me to deflect these requests is to say that I have no authority to perform weddings in Morocco. The U.S. Embassy does not give legal status for weddings and I cannot do this either. People have to get legally married and then I can officiate at a church wedding.

There are other pastors who are more willing to perform weddings and view it as an opportunity to share Jesus with the couple getting married. One pastor who had made an arrangement to officiate at a wedding in Marrakech was deported and asked if I would fulfill his commitment for him. So I traveled to Marrakech, stayed overnight at a beautiful riad[48] with a gorgeous swimming pool. I met with the couple, shared my understanding of marriage, and performed the wedding. I stayed for a bit of the reception and then left with a sense that they were waiting for me to leave so the fun could begin.

MISSIONS—PROSELYTISM—EVANGELISM

MISSIONARIES

Missionaries are a significant part of most international churches. Some international churches are dominated by missionaries, others have just a few, but I would imagine it would be difficult to find an international church that did not have any missionaries as part of the congregation.

What Is a Missionary?

"Missionary" is a loaded term in a country like Morocco. Those who come to this country as missionaries hide this fact from the Moroccan authorities (who nonetheless have it pretty well figured out anyway). When I have been interviewed by the Moroccan equivalent of the American FBI, I have been asked if there are missionaries who come to our church.

I told them that a missionary is someone who is sent to share his or her faith. The Bible tells Christians to share their faith. The Koran tells Muslims

---

[48] A riad is a traditional Moroccan house or palace with an interior garden or courtyard. The word *riad* comes from the Arabic term for garden.

to share their faith. So every good Christian is a missionary and every good Muslim is a missionary. The question is not if I share my faith but whether or not I do it inappropriately. Proselytism in Morocco is more strictly defined as taking advantage of someone's youth, poverty, or lack of education to share your religious beliefs. I agree that is inappropriate. Most parents would be highly offended if someone was sharing their faith with their children without their permission.

I said that if someone asks me on the train if I am a Muslim and I tell them I am a follower of Jesus and a conversation ensues, that is not proselytism. When I receive an email from someone wanting to know more about Jesus, answering the email is not proselytism.

And then, I told the police, "While we are talking, there are Moroccan Muslims on the streets of Europe and the streets of the U.S. sharing their faith, handing out literature about Islam. If I stood out on the street and began to give out information about Christian faith, you would arrest me and send me out of the country within twenty-four hours. Is that fair?"

Periodically I receive an email from someone telling me they have been called by God to convert Muslims to Christianity and want to do this with me in our church. I am aware that my communications may be viewed by Moroccan authorities, but when I respond, I do not respond to cover myself. I respond with what I believe to be true.

I tell the person that we do not do that here. We do not convert anyone. If I am organizing a picnic and tell one person to bring the food, another the drinks, another to arrange transportation, another to organize games, and then tell someone to make sure it does not rain, who has been given the impossible task? It is not in our power to make it rain or be sunny and it is not in our power to convert anyone.

If I use my charisma and intelligence to cause someone to say they want to be a Christian, what have I accomplished? There may be another person added to the role of a church, but has a new name been written in the *book of life*? Any change that has eternal significance is made by God. All I am capable of doing is loving people in the name of Jesus. I love people in his name and when I am asked about why I do what I do, I am ready to give an answer.

As followers of Jesus, we are all missionaries and we go out into the community, into the world to love people in his name and then we step back in amazement as we see how God was able to use our actions and our words for his purposes.

Difficulty of Working with Missionaries

I have not had any major issues with missionaries at our church and have great appreciation for their calling and sacrifice. But as I talked with other international pastors, I discovered that churches with a large percentage of missionaries have difficulties I do not experience. One international pastor told me that missionaries are like manure. Put them together and they cause a big stink. Spread them out and they do great good.

By nature, missionaries tend to be strong-willed, independent, and determined. It takes a certain character to leave the familiarity and comfort of home and head out into the world. A missionary once told David Packer, "Sometimes people complain that we missionaries are not very nice, but the nice people don't last out here. The stubborn ones do."[49]

In a short but brilliant and powerful book that should be required reading for every missionary in the world, David Bosch writes:

> Only too often the possible realization of failure is suppressed and then manifests itself in obstinacy and self-righteousness. Small wonder that the same Hendrik Kraemer whom I have quoted earlier once said: "Communities of missionaries are amongst the most difficult ones in the world!" An American missionary in Rhodesia/Zimbabwe wrote home: "The greatest trial so far has come in getting along with our fellow missionaries."
>
> I suppose one of the reasons for this is that, even in our comfortable modern world, it still takes some guts to become a missionary. Not everybody has the courage to go off to another country to do such a difficult job. So missionaries, by and large, tend to be strong personalities, as they themselves would like to put it. The strength of these personalities may reveal itself in the most peculiar ways, though, for missionaries often conjugate the expression "to be firm" as follows: I am firm, you are stubborn, he is pigheaded. The three words have the same factual meaning; they have, however, very different *emotional* meanings.[50]

Missionaries tend to come to a country with a very set idea of how they will do things. In particular, many young missionaries come convinced they

49 Packer, *Look Who God Let into the Church*, 48.
50 David J. Bosch, *A Spirituality of the Road* (Scottdale, PA: Herald Press, 1979), 45.

will be the first people in the history of the church to do things right. They have read of the failures in the history of church missions. They have been trained by experts and some are not very teachable.

Some go off by themselves and form their own community. This may be because they do not want to be identified with the international church. The thinking seems to be that they have come covertly and do not want their cover to be blown. Others do this as a church planting strategy, expecting that their small house church will invite an interested Moroccan and then another and soon the house church will be a Moroccan house church. Despite the fact that this strategy has not been successful here in Morocco in the last fifty years, people still try.

My approach is to love missionaries, serve them, and be patient. With time they may be drawn into the life of the church. One group discovered that they had too high a rate of turnover because working, eating, playing, and worshiping together as a small team was too claustrophobic. After a few years of team members leaving prematurely, the head of this group made a change in policy and began to encourage the team members to come to the international church and this made their group much healthier.

Regardless of what missionaries think, they need the international church. Their children benefit from the Sunday School and youth programs. They benefit from the fellowship and support they receive. The relationships with people outside their group make their work within their team less claustrophobic.

I am grateful for their presence in our church. They contribute to the high peer level of the church. And I respect their sacrifice and obedience to what God has called them to do.

It is important as pastor not to have expectations of what missionaries or anyone else will do in an international church. I am grateful for any time and service someone wants to give to our church. I realize that if missionaries become too involved in the work of the international church, they may be violating the contract with their supporters who have sent them here. Still, a measure of involvement is helpful to both them and to the church.

Ken MacHarg (Latin America, Europe, Central Asia) adds his perspective:

> Regrettably there are often serious conflicts between missionaries and others—particularly business people. I have seen tension in most churches where there is a large number of missionaries. Too often an influx of these has led to an out-flow of business people and diplomats. Trying to balance this is often a problem that needs to be addressed

openly and with compassion. As you say, missionaries are strong-willed people with a call and too often a dogmatic perspective on what should be preached, how it should be preached, what the church should do, etc. I should know, my wife and I are retired missionaries.

David Packer (Singapore, Stuttgart) shares his experience:

"Missionaries"—your words are spot on! Most of the missionaries we had in our church in Singapore were positive influences, but not all. Some of our biggest problems were started by missionaries who wanted to take control of the church. We had an unwritten policy that no missionary would serve as a deacon in IBC Singapore. We did it on the positive basis of Acts 6—to release them to serve as God called them—but there were also some bad experiences behind the decision as well.

EVANGELISM

If RIC were to begin a door-to-door evangelistic campaign, we would not last long in this country. But we are still called by God to share our faith. How do we do that? Our circumstances push us to a model that I believe is a model for national as well as international churches in settings like ours.

Lesslie Newbigin writes in *The Gospel in a Pluralist Society*: "Almost all of the great Christian preachings in Acts are made in response to a question. Something has happened which makes people aware of a new reality, and therefore the question arises: What is this reality? The communication of the gospel is the answering of that question."[51]

The commotion at Pentecost, the healings and casting out of demons, and the boldness of the disciples all led to questions being asked and then answers being given. We are called to live our lives in such a way that questions are raised. But it is far easier to run down the street shouting out answers to questions no one is asking, and this is what far too many Christians do. The reason for this is that it is far easier to shout out answers than to live your life so questions are raised. When we care for the poor and disenfranchised, when we take up the cause of injustice, when we care for those society has abandoned, when we show compassion to those at our workplace, questions are asked. Then we can share the answer for why we do what we do.

In Morocco we love people in the name of Jesus. We cannot convert them. We do what we are capable of doing—loving them as Jesus has loved us—and

---

[51] Lesslie Newbigin, *The Gospel in a Pluralist Society* (Grand Rapids, MI: Eerdmans, 1989), 132.

then we trust that Jesus will do his work and are grateful that we have been privileged to be a part of his work.

A short-term team visited Morocco and took a train from Rabat up to one of the cities in the interior. That night I sat at a table with them as they each shared about the people they had been able to talk with on the train and how they had been able to talk about Jesus. At the end I asked them if they were this intentional about sharing their faith in their community in the U.S. There was dead silence.

In Morocco, as in every other country of the world, including one's home country, we are called to work with Jesus, loving people in his name and being ready to answer the questions that will arise.

SAND CASTLE MINISTRY

When I was a boy, my family went to the southern New Jersey coast every summer for two or three weeks of vacation and one of the things we loved to do was build sand castles. These were nothing like the elaborate sculptures you see on the news periodically, just a simple structure. We would start with plastic pails of sand to make the base and then drip wet sand to make turrets. We might put sea shells on the walls to decorate the castle and then we would build as large a wall as we could around the castle to protect it from the rising tide of the ocean. But no matter how hard we tried, the waves came closer and closer and then overcame the walls and destroyed the castle.

Ministry in an international church is a sand castle ministry. Over the years I have seen various ministries at RIC thrive and then wash away. Sunday School can run very well with little or no input from me and then the person leading the Sunday School classes will leave and I have to get more involved. We had people leading our weekly prayer meeting and there was a wonderful spirit with praise and worship as well as prayer. But then the two leaders left and the prayer meeting disintegrated to two or three people and then faded away for a time.

I am currently in my best years as pastor of RIC with a strong team that supports me. This team has elevated the ministries of the church so that more people feel loved and cared for and more people feel a part of the church community than ever before. But someday the tide is going to come in and these people will leave. It is very disheartening to anticipate this. Worship may become more simple and I will lead with just my guitar. Perhaps with our move into our new villa we have reached a new level and this will not happen again. But if it does, the transition will be a good news/bad news story. The bad news will be that we lose good worship leaders or teachers, but the good news will be that we are so firmly held in the present that we very quickly get used to the changes that are made. We adapt so quickly to change it amazes me.

David Pederson (Athens, Seoul) gives this illustration:

> One joy of high turnover is that concert pianists, brilliant worship leaders, scholarly teachers, and effective managers continue to show up on my doorstep. However, if too many programs are placed into these capable hands, the result is a gaping hole when the departure comes. Jill was passionate about networking, so she administered the choir, the Sunday School, and volunteer recruitment. Virtually every program outside of the worship service was filled by people that she had enlisted through her persistence and positive spirit. However, when she left, it took two years for the church to recover. Now we limit leadership to one major or two minor involvement areas.[52]

David Packer (Singapore, Stuttgart) gives this illustration:

> During these years [1992-1996] the Promise Keepers organization in the USA had its impact on our church. Several men were interested in beginning a men's ministry and for more than a year we had several groups that met regularly. The ones who were most committed to it and were the leaders were Americans who worked for the State Department who were working on designing the new American Embassy. When their work was completed they were transferred elsewhere, and the men's groups faded just as quickly.[53]

SOCIAL MINISTRY

OUTREACH

My wife and I supported children through World Vision for all of our married life, but when we came to Morocco we ended our support. We still had great respect for World Vision, but now we were in a position to help people directly and no longer needed a middleman.

Using similar logic, when I arrived at RIC I thought we did not need outreach ministries because we were the outreach. But I have learned that even a church on the front line needs to have outreach or it will become indrawn. The church of Jesus Christ must always be reaching out, extending the love of Jesus to the world around it. This is how a church functions best.

---

[52] Pederson, *Expatriate Ministry*, 99.
[53] Packer, *Look Who God Let into the Church*, 29.

RIC became involved with a home for abandoned children and made five bus trips a year to help with building projects at this home. RIC also raises funds to buy school backpacks and supplies for distribution to poor children in September and funds to distribute new baby packages to new mothers in maternity clinics set up for poor women. Raising the funds and doing the distribution is an important part of what we do as an international church.

MIGRANTS

Morocco sits at the northernmost part of the continent of Africa. From the shores of Morocco, you can look over the Straits of Gibraltar to the coast of Spain. This makes Morocco a stepping-off point for migrants of African countries who want to go to Europe.

During my fifteen years of experience with illegal migrants, I have met good men and women who set out on their journey from sub-Saharan Africa with good intentions to find a job that would allow them to send money back home to their family. They make the treacherous trek across the Sahara Desert and into Oujda in Morocco. They arrive in Rabat without their passport (this prevents them from being deported) and without money. The 1,000 euros they thought would get them to Spain has been taken by smugglers and robbers and now another 1,500 euros has to be raised to be smuggled into Spain.

How do they get this money? They call back home and try to get people they know to send more money. They call people they know who are already in Europe and ask them for some money. It is a desperate struggle and so there is, for most migrants, a drift into illegal activities.

Women who start out with the intention of working as maids are forced to prostitute themselves to get across the desert and then, often, their way to Europe is paid for by gangs who will put the women into prostitution once they arrive in Europe and profit from them.

I knew a man who made it to Rabat and then was here for a long time, trying to gather the money he needed to make it to Spain. He was a regular attender at our prayer meetings and at church. He became sick and I helped him get into a hospital. When I went to collect his clothes and passport, I discovered he was earning money by finding men who wanted a prostitute and bringing them to a pimp who had several women staying in an apartment.

If you had asked him when he left Nigeria if he would ever do this, he would have said absolutely not, but as he made his way, he took small step after small step that led him to doing what he never thought he would do. The journey pulls people further and further away from obedience to God.

Part of the destructiveness of this journey is encouraged by a popular teaching in some churches in Africa that says it is all right to deceive people to get to where God is calling you to go. The biblical basis for this is in Exodus when Moses and Israel left Egypt, telling the Pharaoh they were going for just a few days and took the gold and silver of Egypt with them.

This is terrible exegesis and encourages people to use biblical images for their illegal journey to Europe. They say that they will go to Melilla (one of the two Spanish cities along the coast in the north of Morocco) and just like Moses parted the Red Sea, God will part the guards so they can walk into the Promised Land. In this journey, God becomes a tool to be used to get them to where they want to go. They believe that if they pray enough and read their Bible enough, God will bless them and help them get into Spain. RIC has received seed money and seed jewelry that is put in the offering so God will give them money.

There is a lot of deceit. When I have helped someone, the word is passed around about what I did. When I helped someone out because his wife and child were stuck at the Algerian border, within the next couple weeks there were several others with a similar story. I learned over time the importance of checking out these stories. When someone would come to my office telling me he was from Sierra Leone and needed help because he was a refugee and had fled the civil war being fought, I would pick up my phone and call a man in the church who was from Sierra Leone. He would talk to them and then tell me they did not know anything about Freetown, did not know how to speak the pidgin English of Sierra Leone, and, in fact, were from Nigeria. This happened over and over again.

Another time a man from the church came to tell me he had met a woman with a baby who was thinking of killing the baby because she had no way to take care of it. So I went with him to an apartment to meet this woman. When we stepped inside, there was a hallway with four doors. As we waited, the doors opened up and in each room there was a number of women. Finally a man came out and introduced himself. He was wearing gold and platinum chains. We went into one of the rooms with him. There were four mattresses on the floor with seven women sitting watching TV. Three or four of them were holding babies. We sat and talked. I asked him what he was doing in Rabat. He told me he was a student. I asked him who all these women were and he said they needed a place to stay and he was helping them out. I asked where he got the money for the apartment and he told me people from Nigeria sent him money. I told him sarcastically that he was wonderful to be so generous to all these women.

Over the years we have experienced illegal migrants who used their position of serving the church as a means of raising funds to go illegally to Europe. We do not believe this is right and we do not intend to support this illegal move. For this reason it is our church policy not to allow illegal migrants to sing in the choir or usher or in any other way serve in the church. They are welcome to worship with us but are not permitted to serve. It is our judgment that the illegal movement across borders, in particular from sub-Saharan Africa to Spain, is a spiritually destructive journey and we do not want to support that.

If the goal is to fill up the church, then working with these migrants is one of the easiest ways to do this. But the ministry of the church will then be primarily focused on the needs of this community. There are constant requests for money for food and rent from migrants, despite the fact that they are steadily collecting the money they need for passage to Spain. Since they do not have legal status and cannot open a bank account, they store the money in their socks or underwear. So they may be walking around with 800 or 900 euros, but will not eat for days rather than deplete this money they are collecting.[54]

Let me say, after all of this, that I have known several illegal migrants for whom I have had great respect. I know they are in a very difficult position and I can't say what I would have done if I were in their situation. So while we have a church policy about illegal migrants serving in the church, we do not make a judgment that illegal migrants are all bad people. There are many good people stuck in this situation. We are not trying to condemn illegal migrants, but to encourage them to make the wise choice of going back home and seeking legal ways to advance themselves.

The sub-Saharan African students in our church were pleased when the illegal migrants stopped attending in such large numbers. The migrants were constantly trying to strike up relationships with the Westerners in the congregation so they could get some money. This caused the Westerners to be wary of all the Africans, including the legitimate students. The Westerners had a difficult time distinguishing between those who were illegal and those who were students.

Now that we have fewer illegal migrants who come to church, the fellowship in our church has improved. More relationships across racial lines are being

---

[54] I know of two migrant pastors who agreed to hold money for the members of their churches who were saving to pay a smuggler to get across into Spain. When they had enough to pay for their own illegal passage to Spain, the pastors took the money and left.

made. There is a higher sense of trust among us. Ministry to illegal migrants would cost us the ministry we have to our diverse congregation.

Other pastors in Morocco take a different position. One pastor is very active in reaching out to the migrants. He raises funds and takes supplies out to the camps where they live while trying to find a way to get into Spain. He takes the opportunity to preach and teach the truths of Jesus. I am glad he is doing this but I cannot justify it for myself.

Chris Martin (Casablanca) offers a different perspective:

On the section of migrants I think there is a second side to the story and that is those who come here but instead of encountering a downward spiral come to Christ in an international church and get discipled and grow in grace. You also need to think about how you and RIC will now deal with migrants that get legal status in Morocco. We already have many that have received their recipese (residency). For us—we have not allowed migrants to serve on the board or to preach or teach, but those are the only restrictions. And I think those are the only church positions that Biblically call for a higher level of qualification. Now for those who sing—our qualification is that they are saved and living morally (in other words they cannot be living in a sexual relationship unless they are legal married). Because they are in front of the church they need to have a moral lifestyle and be a committed Christian.

Our vision is not to focus on the corruption but on the high potential for the Kingdom of God. For those living in the forest it is first a matter of mercy. Helping the least of the least who are near us. It is second a spiritual matter—showing them the love of God and proclaiming to them that God has a good plan for their lives.

We also strive to preach that right decisions and right living will (generally) lead to true blessing. So, though it may be hard for them—going home is the best thing to pursue God's plan. We are now partnering with IOM (International Organization for Migration) to help migrants return and when they return to get into an assistance program that gets them back into real life in their home country.

Another positive aspect of the migrants is that I do not think CIPC (Casablanca) would exist if it were not for migrants. Today we are a very diverse congregation, but when I became pastor it had shrunk to almost nothing and it was the migrants that built the church. TTC (Tangier) had a great start but fell apart in 2010 and went to zero but was rebuilt by migrants. As we launch MMC (Marrakech), after two months our only committed members are migrants. So, though there may be a lot of corruption in their midst, without these saints the international churches (at least CIPC, TTC, and MMC) would be vastly different if they existed at all.

Another thing you may want to consider is that corruption is much broader than the migrant community and you may have upstanding- looking people in your church who are much more wicked than the average migrant. The French church had a member who was involved in the church but was running a scam of making West African footballers pay him a fee for placing them on a team. These families collected money for their kids. The kids would arrive in Morocco, give this man 1500 euros and their passport, and he did NOTHING for them. He kept their money and sold their passports and had no connection to any football associations in Morocco.

Isn't international church work fun!!!!

CHAPTER FOUR

BENEFITS OF AN INTERNATIONAL CHURCH

UNITY

The unity of the church is a driving concern of God throughout biblical history. Without this awareness we cannot explain God's reaction to the three-hundred-year civil war between Israel and Judah. Jesus' teaching on divorce, Paul's concern with the factions in the church in Corinth, the lists of negative behaviors in Paul's letters—these make sense only when we see God's heart for unity in the church. (I encourage you to read the appendix that discusses this in more detail.)

Once again, this is where international churches shine. We discover unity in the midst of a diverse community. God works to build, create, unite. The devil works to destroy, kill, and divide. In an international church we are working with God to bring unity to the diverse community he is creating.

Ken MacHarg (Latin America, Europe, Central Asia) shares his experience:

> Churches that exist under adversity (as we found in Honduras which is plagued by violence and uncertainty and Kyrgyzstan where religious freedom does not exist and Christians are deported regularly) are usually more united in purpose and calling, focused on ministry, and display less dissatisfaction or divisive "opinions" within their membership. Those, on the other hand, where there is less external adversity or threat or uncertainty exhibit more discord and difference of purpose.

A MORE PURE AND COMPLETE GOSPEL

The process of focusing on the core of our faith involves stripping away the cultural additions to the gospel. Every culture attaches itself to the gospel but we cannot see those attachments. It is like asking a fish about water. Only a creature that is sometimes in water and sometimes not can tell what water is. In the same way, those outside of our culture can see our own cultural attachments.

I have learned that the American gospel is highly individualistic, highly materialistic and I have learned that by being in Bible studies and friendships with brothers and sisters in Christ from other cultures. I have discovered how deeply my American perspective has influenced my view of world events. Over the years this has made me less American and more Christian and that is a good thing. My view of the body of Christ extends far beyond the borders of the U.S.

As others help me see the cultural attachments to the gospel I came to Morocco with, I have been able to focus more intensely on the core of the gospel which has been made richer from what I have learned about the gospel from brothers and sisters in Christ from different cultures.

David Packer (Singapore, Stuttgart) comments:

> Personally I believe in the international church there is greater opportunity to strive for a purer kingdom culture than in most churches in mono-cultural environments.[55]

FOCUS ON THE CORE

In an international church we focus on the core of our faith. Denominations each have a part of the truth but each denomination is weak in some aspect of God's truth. So when we gather together and break denominational, racial, socio-economic, and national lines, we experience more of the unity God wants for us to experience.

During Christmas 2003 I read through the Gospel of Mark in preparation for a series of sermons from Mark. As I read I was astounded because over and over again Jesus healed and cast out demons. I had read Mark many, many times over the years but I had missed this emphasis. The reality is that I had an evangelical filter through which I read the Bible and I relegated these healings and exorcisms to the time of Jesus.

I used to drive past an Assemblies of God church and think to myself, "That is where the crazy Christians go." But when I moved to Rabat, I discovered that some of the people I most admired were from the Assemblies of God. I

---

[55]   Packer, *Look Who God Let into the Church*, 74.

have benefitted from the influence of Pentecostals and while I do not speak in tongues, I am much more open to the work of the Holy Spirit in my life and have a greater expectation that God will work in my life and in the life of others around me.

Pentecostals and Evangelicals need each other and become more complete when they are allowed to influence each other. This is the message of a book written by Paul Cain and R.T. Kendall titled *The Word and the Spirit*. Evangelicals have had an emphasis on the Word of God and Pentecostals on the Spirit of God. The authors talk about the benefit as the Word and Spirit are united.[56] This is what happens in an international church like RIC.

We focus on the core of the faith but that core becomes expanded as we have a more full understanding of the truths in the core.

A PREVIEW OF HEAVEN

What does the Bible say heaven will be like? There are many images and metaphors so we really don't know, but there are a few things we do know for sure. God will be present with us (not to be taken for granted because in Islam, Allah will not be present) and heaven will be populated by people from all the nations from all of time. Revelation 14:6, "Then I saw another angel flying in midair, and he had the eternal gospel to proclaim to those who live on the earth—to every nation, tribe, language and people."

There will not be a Baptist heaven, a Mandarin heaven, a white heaven. Every nation, every tribe, every language, every people will be in heaven. In an international church we are getting practice for how it will be for eternity.

HEALTHY PLACE FOR A PASTOR

In *Lake Wobegon Days*, Garrison Keillor wrote his 95 Theses, complaints of his upbringing in Lake Wobegon, which he intended to nail to the door of the Lutheran Church the night of Halloween, October 31. Here is an excerpt from number 34:

> Actually, I am starved for a good word, but after the long drought of my youth, no word is quite good enough. "Good" isn't enough. Under this thin veneer of modesty lies a monster of greed. I drive away faint praise, beating my little chest, waiting to be named Sun-God, King of America, Idol of Millions, Bringer of Fire, The Great Haji, Thun-dar

---

[56] I highly recommend you read *Empowered Evangelicals: Bringing Together the Best of the Evangelical and Charismatic Worlds* by Rich Nathan and Ken Wilson.

The Boy Giant, I don't want to say, "Thanks, glad you liked it." I want to say, "Rise, my people. Remove your faces from the carpet, stand, look me in the face."[57]

This is the monster of our human nature we try so hard to conceal. We crave the approval of others. And we like to sit on our accomplishments. When the men of a church meet for a Saturday morning Bible Study, there is a silent recognition of who is most successful. The men have a good idea of who makes the most money, who has the most prestigious position, who has the most power. When pastors get together it is not any different. Pastors know whose church has the most members, who has written articles and books, who sits on the most important committees. (This is what some call the three Bs: Building, Budget, Baptisms.) There are some pastors who give in to this worldly perspective and find their worth through their accomplishments but all of us struggle with the temptation.

One of the wonderful aspects of being pastor of an international church is that no matter how well you preach, people leave. And no matter how poorly you preach, people still come. Being pastor of an international church is much less performance-based than in national churches.

Another beneficial aspect of being an international church pastor is that because of the high transition rate in an international church, we are forced to live in the present, not in the past. As I said earlier, if I were to leave RIC after fifteen years of service as pastor, in three years I would be unknown by all but a small percentage of those attending RIC.

We rent a building for our church and in ten years it could well be RIC will be renting another building. We do not have a permanent edifice. But what we have is a long string of relationships and this is what is so helpful about international churches. Buildings come and go and will all be left behind when this world ends, but relationships will move with us into eternity. The fact that an international church places more importance on these relationships is a blessing.

HIGH PEER LEVEL OF SPIRITUAL MATURITY

I like to say that churches around the world pick their best Christians and send them to Rabat which gives me the opportunity to preach to an all-star congregation. The peer level in our church is extraordinarily high and I do not

---

[57] Garrison Keillor, *Lake Wobegon Days* (New York: Viking, 1985), 263.

have to do a lot of exhortation in my preaching. In my preaching, I find myself focusing on encouraging people who are already living their lives for Jesus.

This also makes an international church a great place to preach. I like to say that an all-star congregation takes a mediocre sermon and makes it a good one and they take a good sermon and make it a great one. I do not preach to people who are bored and who come to church because that is the culture. I preach to people who want to come to church, look forward to coming to church, and who want to praise, worship, and hear the Word of God spoken to them.

For someone who comes to the church from a theologically moderate church background, this gives them exposure to many who are committed to Jesus. Over and over again I have seen these people encouraged to grow in their faith and to realize that Christian faith is more than going to church. People discover that Christian faith is a personal relationship with Jesus and they are encouraged to move in that direction by the example of those around them.

MINORITY IN DOMINANT RELIGIOUS CULTURE

Many people tell me that their years at RIC had a very significant effect on their spiritual life. In the years they attend RIC, people draw closer to God and grow in their faith. There are several reasons why I think this is the case.

I just mentioned the high peer level of our church. That is a significant boost to the faith of those who come to RIC. A second factor is the fact that we live in a country that is 99 percent Muslim. When the church is a minority faith living in a dominant Muslim, Hindu, or Buddhist country, the church members are reminded constantly that they are not Muslim, Hindu, or Buddhist. I am more aware that I am a follower of Jesus, different from those around me. This awareness of my identity helps me to be more aware of my relationship with Jesus throughout the week.

A third reason for the boost in faith is that we live outside of the culture of Christmas and Easter. Because of this, the truth of what we celebrate during Christmas and Easter, the birth, death, and resurrection of Jesus, become more pronounced.

When I was in the U.S., the major holiday was Christmas and Easter was a minor holiday. When the culture of these two holidays is stripped away, Easter becomes, at least for me, the better of those two celebrations.

In the U.S., the "Christmas spirit" begins to show up even before Thanksgiving at the end of November. People begin buying Christmas presents, the house is decorated with traditional decorations, Christmas trees are bought, work slows down, and people are let off early from work the days before

Christmas and there is not a lot of work done after Christmas up to New Year's Day.

Here in Morocco, although the stores are increasingly carrying Christmas lights and bulbs and artificial trees, it is not culturally significant. Because it is not a holiday, one Christmas morning our service had to compete with the jackhammers working on the street outside the church. I miss the relaxed atmosphere of Christmas and I miss not being with family during Christmas. We tend not to take time out for Christmas other than December 24 and 25 and quickly slip back into our regular routine.

While Christmas is always a bit underwhelming to me, Easter week is the most wonderful week of the year here in Rabat. We begin with a Palm Sunday service, then come back together on Thursday for a Seder Meal. Friday night we have a Good Friday service during which we nail our names to a cross to make the point that Jesus died for us. Sunday morning we get up early and go to the side of the Chellah (third-century Roman ruins surrounded by twelfth-century walls) for our Sunrise Service. We sit by the side of the valley, sing praises, hear the Easter story, hear someone tell their own story of how Jesus is still resurrecting us, and then sit in silence watching the sheep and cows and birds. Storks fly back and forth with twigs for their nests and we watch the sun come up across the valley. We then head over to our house for an Easter morning breakfast. After enjoying that food and fellowship, we go to church and bring flowers to decorate the cross on which we nailed our names on Friday night. There is a wonderful restorative rhythm to that week that leads us to authentically respond to "He is risen!" with "He is risen indeed!"

PEOPLE IN TRANSITION CAN BE MORE OPEN TO THE GOSPEL AND SPIRITUAL GROWTH

When people leave their home and culture and step into a foreign land and a foreign culture, they can become more reflective about what they believe. Their assumptions about how things are done or why people act as they do are shaken up and they have to think why it is they believe what they do. They no longer have the routines of their home community.

Because of the transitional dynamic of an international church, it does not get stuck in the past. David Packer, who served as pastor of the International Baptist Church of Seoul, observes that in many national churches,

> Long-termers are more important than short-termers . . . the local church must be measured by the standard of the people who are

always going to be around. The problems this perspective causes are several: newcomers are considered second-class citizens, new ideas are seen as inferior to old ideas, and looking backward is more common than looking forward. This attitude definitely deters growth.[58]

This is not a problem most international churches have. Because the overwhelming majority of the people in international churches are transitory, there is more openness to new people, more openness to what comes next, more openness to styles of worship, more openness to what God wants to do in our lives.

This leads to a deeper and more satisfying ministry for an international pastor. David Pederson points out that, "The members are serious about being Christians overseas. Only those who want to maintain fellowship actually make themselves do it because the cultural pressure isn't there. Nobody knows if you go to church or the bar, really."[59]

David Pederson (Athens, Seoul) gives this illustration:

James gripped my hand and smiled, "Living in Korea gave me a lot of surprises, but I never expected that I would find God here." I probed, "So what's the next step?" "Well, I return to London in a fortnight. Can you help me find a church like yours?" I made some suggestions and then asked him what made the international congregation so significant to him. He responded that relevant worship services, the absence of class distinctions, and the emphasis on personal responsibility to follow God's word were factors that showed that the church cared about his spiritual growth. I told him, "Surely there must be some churches in a city that large that can help you." His response was a missiological gem, "Sometimes God has to move you across the world to help you find something that was only a block away."[60]

Roger Hesch (Rabat) comments:

When I remember specific individuals from the international church setting, I realize that, for the most part, my interactions with them were just a small snapshot of their whole persons. That is kind of

---

[58] Packer, *Look Who God Let into the Church*, 6-7.
[59] Pederson, *Expatriate Ministry*, 73.
[60] Pederson, *Expatriate Ministry*, 23.

an awkward statement. What I mean is that the international church setting is almost like an interlude in life for most people. The postings of many workers in an international setting either are for relatively short durations, one to three years years before they return to their home country, or require them to rotate from country to country on a two- to three-year basis. Thus, when I interact with them, I see them only in a point in time without the benefit of their history (save what they share with me).

I have seen this repeated "new beginning" be of great benefit for some people as it allows them to leave behind old habits and negative patterns of life (such as some from military backgrounds developed while living in isolated situations) or return to patterns that they had perhaps developed in childhood or while growing up in church but had left behind as they became involved in other aspects of life. With a positive international church experience I get to see them at their "best" and thus have memories of them as they perhaps would like to be remembered.

PEOPLE FROM PERSECUTED COUNTRIES ARE MORE FREE TO RESPOND TO THE GOSPEL

Morocco cares a lot about protecting the Muslim faith of its citizens but is not really concerned about those who come from other countries. So those who come to Morocco from other Muslim nations or China can feel more free to explore the questions they have about Jesus. We have had people from Asia and Africa who came to Morocco and made a commitment to follow Jesus.

One example of this is also a wonderful story of the globalization of our world. A man from Finland became a follower of Jesus at an international church in China. His company later posted him to Morocco where he befriended a man from China and helped lead him to Christ.

INFLUENCE ON NATIONAL CHURCH LEADERS

There are international churches that actively church plant in the country where they are located. Living in a Muslim country where that is illegal, this is not an option for us. However, this does not prohibit us from having contact with existing Moroccan house churches, particularly with their leaders. In Morocco, the leaders of house churches have mostly been young men who do not have role models for how to lead, how to preach, how to relate as a husband

and father. International church pastors have been able to do this, however imperfectly, with a number of these leaders.

David Pederson (Athens, Seoul) comments:

> In relation to the indigenous community, the international church can do the following: 1) nurture tentmakers who worship in the international church; 2) offer direct benevolence to people because of the geographic proximity to the needs; 3) the international church can be an example to the indigenous community.[61]

---

[61] Pederson, *Expatriate Ministry*, 41.

CHAPTER FIVE

CHALLENGES OF PASTORING AN INTERNATIONAL CHURCH

In reading through this guide, you may begin to see that there are many challenges in leading an international church. Let me comment on a few of them.

STRESS OF LIVING OVERSEAS

In the section about counseling I talked about the stress of living overseas. I am most often a bit depressed the two or three days before I return to Rabat from a vacation in the U.S. or elsewhere. There could be multiple reasons for this. It could be partially spiritual. It could also be leaving a culture in which I am fluent and heading to a culture where I am an alien. It takes me half a day to a day before I adjust to the new baseline and then I am fine. I do not need to take the time in this guide to talk about the general stress of living overseas, but if you are planning to move overseas, I strongly encourage you to read some of the books that deal with adjusting to living overseas that I footnoted earlier and are listed in the bibliography.

Barry Gaeddert (London) comments:

Another item is the suggestion that more should be done for new international pastors in terms of cross-cultural training. Large multinational corporations have training programs for those going on expat assignments. Certainly a large number of missions organizations have well-defined and well-developed cross-cultural training programs for those who will be new to the field. It would be a good idea for a pastor who is new to international ministry to participate in a training that intentionally addresses cross-cultural issues.

STRESS OF DIVERSITY

In the book of Acts, the Greek-speaking and Hebrew-speaking followers of Jesus quarreled about the distribution of food to widows. However wonderful diversity is, it does not come without tension. Gerard Marks, Pastor of Kobe Union Church, made these comments about the stress of diversity.

Seven generalizations emerge from studies of diversity within congregational life.

First, the greater the degree of diversity, the greater the stress on the minister.

Second, the greater the emphasis on the religious diversity while the greater the emphasis on interpersonal relationships, the more difficult it is to retain that high level of diversity.

Third, the greater the diversity among the members, the more important the need to enhance the group life of the congregation so everyone who feels that need can find a homogeneous unit group or "home" within that diversity. In other words, diversity usually produces complexity. Those who want life to be simple and easy to understand and who prefer the uncomplicated tend to resist expanding the group life in order to accommodate that diversity.

Fourth, the greater the degree of diversity, the more critical the personality of the pastor as a central and unifying force.

Fifth, the greater the diversity, the more disruptive changes in staff leadership tend to be, so longer pastorates should be part of a strategy for enhancing diversity.

Sixth, the greater the degree of diversity, the more essential a consistent "affirm and build" style of leadership by the pastor.

Finally, the greater the degree of diversity among the members, the more likely it will be wise to expect that one result will be a broad and highly varied program with an extremely complex schedule and an exceptionally redundant system of internal communication.[62]

THE PAIN OF SAYING GOODBYE

Every international pastor I speak with tells me about the pain of saying goodbye to members when they leave. I have talked about pastoring an

---

[62] Gerard Marks, summarizing material from Lyle Shaller, *Reflections of a Contrarian: Second Thoughts on the Parish Ministry*, quoted in Pederson, *Expatriate Ministry*, 78.

international church being like pastoring a parade. You extend your hand to greet someone and then slowly lift it up to wave goodbye in too few short years. David Pederson wrote, "I estimate that I have said goodbye to over a thousand regular attendees in our ten years of ministry."[63]

When we say farewell, I have often used a passage from Antoine de Saint-Exupéry's *Wind, Sand, and Stars*. Saint-Exupéry is best known for his book, *The Little Prince*, and flew in the 1920s and 1930s for what later became Air France. In those days, accidents were frequent and Saint-Exupéry writes about the experience of showing up at the airfield and hearing that one more friend had died.

> Bit by bit, nevertheless, it comes over us that we shall never again hear the laughter of our friend, that this one garden is forever locked against us. And at that moment begins our true mourning, which, though it may not be heart-rending, is still slightly bitter. For nothing, in truth, can replace that companion. Old friends cannot be created out of hand. Nothing can match the treasure of common memories, of trials endured together, of quarrels and reconciliations and generous emotions. It is idle, having planted an acorn in the morning, to expect that afternoon to sit in the shade of the oak.
>
> So life goes on. For years we plant the seed, we feel ourselves rich; and then come other years when time does its work and our plantation is made sparse and thin. One by one, our comrades slip away, deprive us of their shade.[64]

While friends in an international church rarely die, their move to a new part of the world is a death experience. How do we react to this? David Packer writes, "[The constant loss of friends] is a challenge to the pastoral and ministerial staff. We get fatigued also dealing with so many people coming and going—a type of compassion fatigue—to where our equilibrium can also be just a bit shaken."[65] Our instinct is to pull in and protect ourselves from pain and be less willing to enter into new relationships so freely, but this works against what we need. We need friends to support and encourage us. When people in the U.S. ask me how they can pray for me, I tell them to pray that I will have the spiritual and emotional strength to stay open to new relationships.

---

[63] Pederson, *Expatriate Ministry*, 96.

[64] Antoine de Saint-Exupéry, *Wind, Sand, and Stars* (London, UK: The Folio Society, 1990), 26.

[65] Packer, *Look Who God Let into the Church*, 49.

So, we say goodbye to friends who have provided us with such wonderful shade and say hello to saplings that walk into the church. What has amazed me is that these saplings, year after year, develop so quickly into trees under whose shade we can relax.

This is a necessary part of the life of a pastor of an international church. Fortunately, the pain of saying goodbye to great friends is matched by the delight of getting to know new, extraordinary people.

CHAPTER SIX

WHAT MAKES A GOOD INTERNATIONAL CHURCH PASTOR?

How do you know if you would be a good international church pastor? There is no perfect international church pastor so if you are not perfect you might be qualified. My point is that there is more than one kind of person who is a good pastor of an international church. Here are two lists of qualities deemed helpful and necessary for international pastors.

Rodney Woo, in *The Color of Church*, lists nine nonnegotiable qualities for multicultural leadership:

1) exposure and experience with multiple races
2) a strong biblical base
3) an evangelistic heart
4) a global vision
5) a teachable spirit
6) a forbearing spirit ("the attitude which gives others permission to be different")
7) advocate of shared diverse leadership
8) seasoned facilitator in conflict resolution
9) person of passionate prayer[66]

David Packer lists four qualities for international church leadership:

    1)   Leadership that lives by the expectation and creates a positive hope for others that something good can come from Christian fellowship that extends itself across cultures and

---

[66] Rodney Woo, *The Color of Church* (Nashville, TN: Broadman, 2009), 205–218.

nationalities. The leadership must do much more than tolerate difference; they must see them as positive.

2)   Leadership councils and representatives that include people from different cultures—meaning that they accept them as different, value them as brothers and sisters in Christ, treat them with respect and consideration, and include them in the fellowship.

3)   Leadership that listens to the concerns and ideas of people from other cultures. We like to be where we are celebrated, not where we are tolerated.

4)   Leadership that also has the good sense to know the limits of their flexibility, to know when, where, and how to draw the line on blending the congregation. There is a danger when leaders naively idealize cultural differences, because in each culture there are elements that the gospel and the Word of God need to confront and change.[67]

I asked international church pastors what qualities are needed to be a good pastor of an international church. This chapter discusses what they told me. First and foremost, an international church pastor needs to love the people he or she serves. This is true of all pastors and is, as I understand it, what the gift of pastor is all about. To be pastor of a community is to have the heart of God for that community. There are many other qualities necessary for the pastor of any church: a good listener, a strong devotional life, etc. but there are some qualities especially needed in ministry in an international church.

CALL TO THE INTERNATIONAL CHURCH

As I was praying prior to moving to Rabat, God gave me a clear sense of call. I was to support those who were here as missionaries; I was to reach out to other expatriates; and I was to support the local church in any way I could. This was very clear and this has continued to be my sense of call over the years. I did not come to Rabat as pastor of RIC as a cover for my work with Moroccans. My call as pastor of RIC was my priority and influenced me in my choice of which language to learn. It was certain that I had to learn either French or Arabic and because my work was going to be with the church, I chose to learn French.

When the pastor of an international church is using the church to cover his or her activities with local believers, then the international church suffers.

---

[67]   David Packer, *Look Who God Let into the Church* (n.p.: Growth Points International, 2013), 13–14.

Ken MacHarg (Latin America, Europe, Central Asia) gives this illustration:

A difficult decision with many consequences both good and bad is whether an international church should primarily minister to and with expatriates or should also develop a ministry to local Christians and an outreach to local non-Christians. Generally speaking, I have found that when the emphasis shifts from expats to and/or primarily local the nature of the church changes. Quite often after a period of time and a large influx of local (new) Christians and the time and emphasis that ministry takes, expats will start to leave and either find or start a new expat-oriented church.

When the Union Church of San Jose, Costa Rica, reoriented its ministry thirty years ago to emphasize local people married to expats and became a bilingual church, and subsequently relocated to the east side of the city, most of the expats left and eventually started a small Sunday school for children that grew into Escazu Christian Fellowship. Both churches continue today as strong congregations, but the old Union Church group is more and more oriented toward local folks while ECF is definitely an expat church. Not that ministry to local people is wrong—but a church must be absolutely clear about what it is doing and consider the consequences and ability to maintain a viable ministry to expats.

Part of my expression here is that I have a strong call from the Lord to minister to expats. I know them and their issues, I know how to preach and minister in that context. Not that I don't love local people—I do and we have very close friends and relationships with many local people in our churches. I just would never want to develop a ministry that ignored the needs of expats.

FLEXIBILITY

A pastor who is rigid and has a definite way of doing things will not be helpful to an international church. Flexibility is demanded by the multiple cultures represented, multiple denominations and theologies represented, and by the continual turnover in the makeup of the community.

NOT DOGMATIC

There are denominational international churches, but even these, I believe, need to be less denominational than their denomination. Because so many theological backgrounds are represented in the church, a pastor who insists on his or her denominational perspectives will unnecessarily alienate people who could be part of the community.

One couple attended a church in Brussels before moving to Rabat. Although they wanted to be active in the ministry of the church in Brussels, they were not permitted to become members because they did not have the gift of speaking in tongues. This was a loss for the church in Brussels. RIC is now benefitting from the friendship and spiritual gifting of this bright, energetic couple.

RELATIONAL

A pastor who is numbers driven (Three Bs—Building, Budget, Baptisms) will be frustrated in an international church. If my ego is based on how the world views success, I will be miserable in an international church. Being pastor of an international church is all about relationships and one of the great blessings is the large number of close friendships with people living around the world, that are formed over time.

It is important to disciple people who come to the international church and the international church will benefit from the growth they experience. But they will leave and it is the churches they will go to in the future who will most benefit from their spiritual growth. An international church pastor needs to value the friendships that will last and freely bless the churches where these friends will go when they leave.

Being a visionary is highly valued in large, national churches, but in international churches that have a vague past and a limited future, this is not as much of an asset. What is highly valuable in an international church is being relational. Building relationships is what matters most in international churches.

ENCOURAGER

Living overseas, away from family, can be very difficult. There is a sacrifice that is made living overseas, away from home, family, and friends. It is not easy living in a country where you don't speak the language fluently enough to feel comfortable. And even if that language proficiency is attained, the culture is still foreign. There is increased stress on marriages. The need for community is increased. So the pastor needs to be an encourager in sermons, in relationships, in the life of the church.

If, as the pastor of the church, you love the flock God has given to you, then it will be easy to encourage people who are generally highly motivated and wanting to live a life that pleases God.

GROUNDED AND SECURE /
OPEN IN RELATIONSHIP WITH GOD

I have had many, many people over the past fifteen years who have laid hands on me and prayed for me to receive the baptism of the Holy Spirit, evidenced by speaking in tongues. I am not offended by this and appreciate their desire for me to receive from God what they believe I need.

I work at being open to God to receive anything he wants for me to have. As I mentioned, when I preach about gifts of the Holy Spirit, I tell the church that it would be a foolish soldier that did not enter battle with everything the sergeant thought would be necessary. I don't want to limit God in any way and whatever gift he wants me to have, I want to have.

As an evangelical, if you come to an international church, you need to not be afraid of or intimidated by those who speak in tongues. In a prayer meeting, when people speak in tongues or sing in the Spirit, you need to be able to be comfortable sitting there and meditating and praying. I actually find it quiet, relaxing, and beautiful. A Pentecostal pastor must also be secure enough to work with and love people who do not agree with Pentecostal theology.

A good international pastor needs to be able to send people to a specialist when it is helpful and not try to do everything him or herself. When someone comes to me with an issue outside of my experience, I send that person to someone in the church with a similar background. I don't need to be the resident expert.

WORLD CITIZEN

Some people come overseas and fall in love with being overseas. They thrive in this environment with so many different cultures. But there are others who tolerate the couple years they have to stay and cannot wait to get back to their home country. This is true even with children in families who spend many years overseas. Some of the children will be world citizens and others cannot wait to get settled and leave their home country only when necessary.

An international church pastor has to be one of those who loves the cultures of the world and thrives in this international environment.

LONGEVITY

Because of the high rate of transition in international churches, it is helpful if the pastor serves for longer periods of time. People have commented frequently, in the past few years, that my long-term presence in Rabat gives them a feeling of security.

ACCOUNTABILITY

For seven years I was part of an accountability group consisting of other pastors and church leaders, but this group fell apart. I am currently rebuilding an accountability group and setting up an accountability relationship with our church in the U.S. It is so important that there be a deep level of accountability where no question cannot be asked. If the pastor of an international church falls (spiritually, ethically, morally), he or she will make a huge splash and damage the work of the church. Many will suffer because one person fell.

ASSOCIATE PASTORS

An associate pastor needs to have the qualities listed above but he or she also needs to have a sense of call to international church ministry. There have been those who have wanted to work with me as a means of getting residency in Morocco so they could do what they really wanted to do, reach out with the gospel of Jesus to Moroccans.

I tell people that they have to have a sense of call to international church ministry. Otherwise, they are using the international church and not serving it. This is true for associate pastors and it is true for pastors as well.

CHAPTER SEVEN

AN INTERACTION WITH TWO INTERNATIONAL PASTORS

When I began working on my DMin in 2010, I did a preliminary search for books that described ministry in international churches and did not find any. As I resumed my search for literature in preparation for this guide, I discovered two books. One was written by David Pederson who served as pastor of international churches in Athens, Greece, and Seoul, Korea. His PhD dissertation, "Choosing Three Worlds: A biblical paradigm of expatriate ministry with practical applications for the English-speaking international congregation," was edited in 1999 into a book: *Expatriate Ministry: Inside the Church of the Outsiders*.[68]

A second book was published in 2013 by David Packer: *Look Who God Let into the Church: Understanding the Nature and Sharpening the Impact of a Multicultural Church*.[69] David Packer served as pastor of the International Baptist Church of Singapore for twelve years and his book speaks mostly about those years. He is currently pastor of the International Baptist Church of Stuttgart, Germany.

My experience as an international pastor has been limited to fifteen years as pastor of Rabat International Church. I have also visited international churches in Rome, Istanbul, Lisbon, and three international churches in Chiang Mai, Thailand—as well as several international churches in Morocco. It has been helpful to see the differences between the churches these pastors served and the church I serve.

---

[68]   David Pederson, *Expatriate Ministry: Inside the Church of the Outsiders* (Seoul, Korea: Korean Center for World Missions, 1999).
[69]   David Packer, *Look Who God Let into the Church* (n.p.: Growth Points International, 2013).

Both of the churches David Packer has served are large, especially from the perspective of international churches. The church in Singapore grew from an average Sunday attendance of 500 to 1,500 during his twelve years as pastor. The church in Stuttgart is currently averaging 700 each Sunday.

Packer lists three international churches from which people could choose in Singapore: Community of Praise (a church start of International Baptist Church which became charismatic); St George's Anglican Church; and IBC.[70] Pederson lists 21 international protestant churches in Seoul.[71]

The church in Singapore had a significant percentage of Singaporeans all through the twelve years Packer was pastor. When it added staff, one addition was Associate Pastor to Singaporeans. In both Athens and Seoul, it was permissible for nationals to attend the international church.

These three dynamics (size, choice, and a significant presence of nationals) have a significant impact on the life and ministry of an international church.

SIZE

The size of a church makes a difference. I talked earlier about ministry in an international church being a "sand castle" ministry. Someone arrives who uses his or her gifts to make a part of church ministry shine and then when they leave, that part of church ministry may or may not continue. If it does, it could function in a less proficient manner. No matter how elaborate the sand castle, the tide of departure flows and the castle disappears.

I mentioned earlier about Packer's experience with a men's ministry inspired by the Promise Keepers organization in the U.S. and how this disappeared when the Americans working for the State Department left.

But as the church grew, the "sand castle" nature of the church disappeared. In 1996, with an average Sunday attendance of 900 and 500 in the Sunday School, Packer noticed a difference:[72]

> After we began averaging around 500 in Bible Study, our programming began to be more consistent. We began to reach the "critical mass" number that meant when someone transferred to another city, the position was filled quickly. Previously we had some

---

[70] David Packer, *Look Who God Let into the Church*, 23.

[71] David Pederson, *Expatriate Ministry*, 160.

[72] The difference between a small, transitional church and other small churches is that transitional churches do not have someone who has led the Sunday School program for twenty-five years. All small churches have disruption in their ministry when a key person leaves/dies, but this is a frequent experience for international churches.

fairly wild swings in the quality of our programming, simply because we did not have the depth of volunteers. For example, someone would start a program and it would work out fine while they were there, but then they would leave and someone without their gifts would try to pick up the program and go forward with it, but was just unable to do it. However, after we reached 500, the wild swings seemed to lessen and the entire quality of programming tended to stabilize.[73]

The two churches Pederson served are more similar in size to RIC so both Pederson and I have faced the inconsistencies of a "sand castle" ministry. There is a positive and negative side to this.

In the Tom Hanks movie *Castaway*, Hanks portrays a FedEx employee whose plane crashes in the South Pacific and he is stranded on an uninhabited island for four years. When he is found and is back in the U.S., he reflects on what he learned over those years: "And I know what I have to do now. I gotta keep breathing. Because tomorrow the sun will rise. Who knows what the tide could bring?"[74]

This is the positive side. Each summer the tide brings new people and we discover their gifts as we enter into the fall. Pederson writes, "One joy of high turnover is that concert pianists, brilliant worship leaders, scholarly teachers, and effective managers continue to show up on my doorstep."[75] I too have experienced the joy of a concert pianist who could play Fernando Ortega's "Sing to Jesus" with just a five-minute run-through and many others with great talents who wanted to use their gifts to serve the church. An international church attracts highly-motivated and highly-talented people.

On the negative side, when these people move on, a vacuum is left in their place. One solution is to limit what talented people could do in the church. This is what Pederson did in not allowing any one member of the church to take on too many responsibilities.

I understand this need to minimize the pain of radical change but I have taken a different approach. I am eager to accept all that any person has to offer, even if that person's departure will mean a significant change in the ministry of the church. I embrace with joy the ministry a person brings even when it feels like I am out on a limb because I know that person will be gone in a year. This

---

[73] Packer, *Look Who God Let into the Church*, 31.

[74] IMDb Castaway Quotes, http://www.imdb.com/title/tt0162222/quotes.

[75] Pederson, *Expatriate Ministry*, 99.

can be a terrifying feeling but I have learned to trust that God will bring new people with new gifts. We may not be the same church but we will continue to be a great church.

I encourage people who are leaving to pass on what they have learned in their area of ministry to someone who expresses interest in taking responsibility after they leave. Whether or not that part of the ministry continues, the church adapts. This is a great feature of an international church with a high rate of transition: in six months to a year, a third to half of the church will not have known that ministry ever existed. The church adapts rapidly to change because it lives so firmly in the present.

CHOICE

One of the pastors David Pederson interviewed said, "Defining the theology of this church is like pinning Jell-O to the wall."[76] This is a reflection of the wide range of theological views present in an international church. Arthur Bauer, former director of an international church organization, listed five characteristics of the international church, the first of which is ecumenical:

> The scope of Christian experience found in international congregations is amazing. Left and right, conservative and liberal, simple and profound, formal and informal, Bible-centered and Bible-ignored, intellectual and earthy, traditional and experimental, name the variety of church expressions and you will be listing a portion of most international congregations.[77]

How does a pastor handle this range of theologies? In Packer's church in Singapore, people could choose which international church to attend. Packer writes, "Those who were neither liturgical nor charismatic tended to prefer IBC."[78] The theological mishmash was minimized because people drifted to the church that more closely reflected their theological view.

But not all those who attend international churches have this choice. Pederson states, "An international pastor stays for about five years. Even in cases where there is obvious cooperation, it is rare to have a pastor remain for longer than seven years in the same position."[79] He then goes on to say, "As

---

[76] Pederson, *Expatriate Ministry*, 53.

[77] Pederson, 36.

[78] Packer, *Look Who God Let into the Church*, 23.

[79] Pederson, *Expatriate Ministry*, 118.

far as the congregation's unity is concerned, turnover in the pastoral position is sometimes necessary to maintain unity among the many denominations represented in a congregation."[80] I don't agree. Three to five years of a Baptist preacher followed by three to five years of an Assemblies of God pastor does not sound like much of a solution to achieve church unity.

The first churches I served as pastor were two small Presbyterian churches (PCUSA) in eastern Ohio. These churches had been subjected to a series of pastors of varying theological perspectives over the years. Pastors who were just starting out, like me, or pastors who had not been able to move on to larger churches came in, preached their sermons, and then moved on, most often after three years or less.

At one point, in an effort to seek renewal of the spiritual life of the church, I asked a group to come to the church for a weekend to inspire the congregation. As part of the process, they asked me to have the church session fill out an informational form and one of the questions they asked was, "Are you theologically liberal, moderate, or conservative?" The session did not know how to answer the question and so I asked them if I was theologically more liberal or conservative than their previous pastor (who was much more theologically liberal than I am). They answered that I was more liberal. I asked why they thought that and they replied that I played the guitar in church. They had been subjected to so many theologies that they had Jell-O theology. Drifting from theology to theology is not helpful. The transitional nature of international churches minimizes this damage, but there is a much better solution.

Albert Bauer defined international churches as being both ecumenical and evangelical. Lay these two characteristics side by side—ecumenical and evangelical—and you can see the potential problem and solution. Will the focus be on our diversity or on Jesus? To focus on Jesus is to focus on the core of our faith. There is no Jell-O to be found in the core. But when we focus on the peripheral issues that divide us, we create confusion and dissension. This is not to say we should avoid truth, simply that truth is found in the core and speculation in the periphery. When we focus on the core of our faith, we focus on what brings us life.

The diversity of an international church is a blessing, not a curse. Pederson asked international pastors what was unique about their international church experience. One pastor responded, "I could go on all day telling you what is unique, but the biggest thing is the blend of denominations and cultures into

---

[80] Pederson, 118.

one church. The focus is upon those things more deep and significant rather than those things which seem so petty and trivial.[81]

I talk about this in the appendix, that when we focus on the core of our faith, we celebrate the diversity of our faith in an experience of unity.

I am grateful that Rabat does not have an English-speaking, Protestant church alternative. People are thrust together and have to deal with the differing theologies, but this leads to a strength, not to a weakness. As a consequence of having all the theologies brought together, along with cultural preferences, we are pushed to focus on the core of our faith and not on the peripheral doctrines that divide us. This means that we spend more time on preaching and teaching that leads to life and less on preaching and teaching that unnecessarily divides.

NATIONALS IN CHURCH

Both Packer and Pederson were pastors of international churches in cities where nationals were permitted to attend. That is a debatable case for RIC. I am told that before I arrived in 2000 there were occasions in which the police entered the church building to take out Moroccans who were attending one of the church services. This has not happened since I have been there, but the general sense has been that because it is illegal to convert to another religion from Islam, the government does not want Moroccans to come to the international church services.

As a consequence, I did not deal with the interaction between nationals and internationals in chapter three. Packer writes about a major conflict in the church in Singapore.[82] Although the church was growing, a conflict arose between the Asians and Westerners about who was leading the church. The "success" of the church raised the stakes and ownership and control became more important. The church grew from 500 to 1,500 and they bought a piece of land and built a new church facility. The needs of Singaporeans who were at IBC for the long-term conflicted with the needs of the Westerners who were transitioning through IBC.

In writing about the Roman church of the New Testament, Pederson makes the point that, "It was not their differences from each other that kept them apart, but their differences from the dominant indigenous culture that kept them together."[83] Singaporean members of IBC were part of the culture

---

[81] Pederson, *Expatriate Ministry*, 39.

[82] Packer, *Look Who God Let into the Church*, 124.

[83] Pederson, *Expatriate Ministry*, 59.

that made the Westerners feel foreign. The pull of the Singaporean culture was much stronger on Singaporeans than on the Westerners so it is obvious why this became a tension. Singaporeans gave to the ministry of the church as did the Westerners, but the Singaporeans remained when the Westerners left. This gave them a stronger sense of ownership and control. The relationship in international churches between internationals and nationals is an area for more exploration.

CHAPTER EIGHT

LESSONS FOR CHURCHES IN THE U.S.

WHY HAVE INTERNATIONAL CHURCHES RECEIVED SO LITTLE ATTENTION?

When I started writing this guide and looked for books and articles that discussed international church ministry, I was surprised to find very few resources. Why have international churches received so little attention? Because my experience and the experience of others who pass through international churches is so rich, it is odd that international churches have not received more attention.

In talking about why the post-WWII generation of missionaries viewed expatriate ministry as substandard Christian mission, David Pederson points out that:

> International congregations were often seen as a social club for the diplomatic and business community who refused to integrate into the host culture. These churches were often encouraged by Western governments and corporations that had a vested interest in keeping their employees from "going native."[84]

It may be true that international churches once functioned as social clubs for the diplomatic and business community and that missionaries were encouraged to avoid these churches because they served as a distraction from their calling to bring the gospel to the nations. But much has changed in the last sixty years.

---

[84] Pederson, *Expatriate Ministry*, 5.

The world has shrunk. In the 1930s a trip by air from London to Singapore took eight days and cost about $18,000 USD. This trip by boat took one month.[85] Today I fly from Rabat to Paris to Bangkok to Chiang Mai, where my daughter and her family live, in less than a day—at a cost of less than $2,000 USD. I can visit for a couple weeks and fly home, all in half the time it took to travel by boat—one way—seventy years ago.

In the 1930s, letters took months to reach their destination. Today, I send an email to anywhere in the world and it takes less than a second to reach its destination. I talk by Skype with friends and family and can actually see them as we talk. It is far less difficult to live overseas than it used to be.

As our world has become smaller, those who attend international churches are no longer only diplomats, businessmen, and intrepid missionaries. Today our church has university students and high school students who come to live and study in Morocco for a semester. The ease with which we travel around the globe makes it far easier for people to spend some years in another country, pursuing a business opportunity, or simply wanting to experience life in another country for a while. Life in another country is a lot more normal than it used to be.

A second reason David Pederson gives for why international church ministry was viewed as substandard is, "Missionaries often treated the international church as a place of refuge rather than outreach."[86]

I can understand this. In order to share the gospel of Jesus with people from a foreign culture, it is first necessary to learn the language and culture of that foreign land. This takes a lot of time and immersion into that culture is necessary. When too much time and energy is spent in an English-speaking community, the acquisition of language slows down and the necessary language skills and cultural understanding may never happen. On the other hand, as I have pointed out in this guide, without the support of an international church, the stress of living in a foreign land often becomes too much and people leave prematurely to go back to their home country. It is clear that a balance is needed.

Nevertheless, it is clear that this bias against international church ministry has continued. There are denominational and parachurch mission agencies that have a policy that discourages their workers from attending international

---

[85] "What International Air Travel Was Like in the 1930s," *Paleofuture*, http://paleofuture. gizmodo.com/what-international-air-travel-was-like-in-the-1930s-1471258414.

[86] Pederson, *Expatriate Ministry*, 5.

churches. They want their workers to meet in house churches that can incorporate local believers.

This bias is also seen in the focus of theses about international church ministry. When international church ministry is the subject for a thesis, the focus is almost always on how an international church can be a springboard for church planting.[87] It seems that the life and ministry of an international church is not valued except for what it can do in the cause of missions.

This is unfortunate because this is an area of church ministry that needs to be encouraged and studied. The world is shrinking and we are closer to our brothers and sisters in Christ than ever before. This is good news and we are blessed when we make the effort to step out of our comfort zone and embrace God's much-loved diverse family.

I have been encouraged and stimulated by reading about multiethnic congregations in the U.S. There is much international church pastors can learn from what these congregations are experiencing. And there is much national churches can learn from international churches. We benefit when we open ourselves to the wisdom and experience of others.

THE INTERNATIONAL CHURCH HAS COME TO THE U.S.

As the world has shrunk, increasingly, the nations of the world have come to the U.S. The U.S. has always been a land of immigrants, but the last two decades have seen a dramatic increase in immigration.

Using data from the 1990 U.S. census, Stephen Rhodes writes,

> From 1980 to 1990, the United States experienced the largest amount of immigration since the turn of the century, as well as the most racially and ethnically diverse ever. In that decade 9.5 million documented and undocumented immigrants arrived in the U.S. Those 9.5 million immigrants represent almost one-fifth of the 54 million immigrants who have come to the United States since 1820.[88]

Since then, the numbers of immigrants to the U.S. have increased even more dramatically.

New data from the Census Bureau show that the nation's immigrant

---

[87] For example, see Joseph Szabo, "Planting International Churches as a Strategy to Reach Immigrants and Expatriates in Western Europe" (doctoral thesis, Assemblies of God Theological Seminary, 2011).

[88] Stephen A. Rhodes, *Where the Nations Meet: The Church in a Multicultural World* (Downers Grove, IL: IVP Academic, 2012), 15.

population (legal and illegal), also referred to as the foreign-born, reached 40 million in 2010, the highest number in American history. Nearly 14 million new immigrants (legal and illegal) settled in the country from 2000 to 2010, making it the highest decade of immigration in American history.[89] Here are some other findings from this report:

- The nation's immigrant population has doubled since 1990, nearly tripled since 1980, and quadrupled since 1970, when it stood at 9.7 million.

- Growth in the immigrant population has primarily been driven by high levels of legal immigration. Roughly three-fourths of immigrants in the country are here legally.

- Immigrants continue to head to non-traditional states of settlement. The six states with the largest immigrant populations accounted for 65 percent of the total in 2010, 68 percent in 2000, and 73 percent in 1990.

- Overall the immigrant population grew 28 percent between 2000 and 2010. But it grew at more than twice the national rate in: Alabama (92 percent), South Carolina (88 percent), Tennessee (82 percent), Arkansas (79 percent), Kentucky (75 percent), North Carolina (67 percent), South Dakota (65 percent), Georgia (63 percent), Indiana (61 percent), Nevada (61 percent), Delaware (60 percent), Virginia (60 percent), and Oklahoma (57 percent).

- Since 1990 the immigrant population has doubled. It grew at more than twice the national rate in: North Carolina (525 percent), Georgia (445 percent), Arkansas (430 percent), Tennessee (389 percent), Nevada (385 percent), South Carolina (337 percent), Kentucky (312 percent), Nebraska (298 percent), Alabama (287 percent), Utah (280 percent), Colorado (249 percent), Minnesota (235 percent), Delaware (223 percent), Iowa (222 percent), Indiana (219 percent), Oklahoma (215 percent), and Arizona (208 percent).

- States with the largest numerical increases over the last decade were: California, Texas, Florida, New York, New Jersey, Georgia, Virginia,

---

[89]   Steven A. Camarota, "A Record-Setting Decade of Immigration: 2000-2010," *Center for Immigration Studies*, posted October 2011, http://cis.org/2000-2010-record-setting-decade-of-immigration.

North Carolina, Maryland, Washington, Illinois, Pennsylvania, and Massachusetts.

- Latin America continued to dominate immigration. Countries from this region accounted for 58 percent of the growth in the immigrant population from 2000 to 2010.

I don't expect anyone to read all these states and their percentages, but each reader will look for his or her state in this list. I share these census findings because they make clear that it is not just the large cities of the coastal states in the U.S. that have taken on more of an international feel; cities and towns across the U.S. have received influxes of immigrants. This is changing the face of the U.S.

Manuel Ortiz writes about the community where he lives in Philadelphia:

When I, as a Puerto Rican, wake up to the hustle and bustle of the African-American community in which I live, I realize that there are similarities and dissimilarities in our lifestyles, yet we live as neighbors. When I go to our favorite grocery store to buy the ingredients to make our regular Puerto Rican meals, I discern that the owners are from an area not associated with Latin America—they are Palestinian. I go to the cobbler shop, and the man who tells me that my shoes will be ready by five o'clock is from Southeast Asia. The hardware store is close by, and I walk over to have an additional set of keys made. The owner speaks to me of her home in Seoul, Korea, in tone suggesting she would like to be there for the summer months.[90]

Leonard Sweet, in his book *FaithQuakes*, says that Americans now eat more tortillas for breakfast than bagels or biscuits or pita bread; more salsa is sold now than ketchup."[91] There is an irony in our changing breakfast habits since bagels came to the U.S. with Jewish immigrants, pita bread came from the Middle East, and even biscuits came with the Europeans who immigrated to North America. We delight in new food but forget that the migration of food has been taking place for a long time.

In *Near a Thousand Tables*, Felipe Fernández-Armesto presents a fascinating history of food and how regional cuisines were affected when two cultures met. The food on our tables is far more international that we think. For example,

---

[90] Manuel Ortiz, *One New People: Models for Developing a Multiethnic Church* (Downers Grove, IL: IVP), 28–29.

[91] Leonard Sweet, *FaithQuakes* (Nashville, TN: Abingdon, 1994), 176.

when we go to an Italian restaurant, we delight in the cuisine of Italy. But Fernández-Armesto reminds us that,

> The Italian tricolor represents the colors of the national flag with slices of tomato, mozzarella and avocado. Mozzarella is the cheese of an indigenous variety of water buffalo. Avocados and tomatoes, however, were fruits Italy got from America.... Equally indispensable items on the Italian menu—gnocchi and polenta—are made from potatoes and maize respectively. Many ingredients now deeply imbedded in other "national" cuisines of European, African, and Asian countries were similarly unknown in their present homelands until the Columbian exchange (the importation of foods from the Americas to Europe).[92]

We delight in the foods of the world. Why do we not delight also in the people who bring them?

THE INTERNATIONAL CHURCH: A CHALLENGE TO THE HOMOGENEOUS UNIT PRINCIPLE

One objection to multiethnic churches is the argument that churches that are diverse do not grow as well as those that are homogenous. When Manuel Ortiz walks through his neighborhood, encountering the nations of the world, what is his responsibility to the African-Americans, the Palestinians, and the Koreans he meets? As a Puerto Rican, he is Hispanic. What is the best strategy for him to reach out to his neighbors with the gospel of Jesus?

Peter Wagner would suggest that Ortiz should focus his energy on a Hispanic church:

> [Wagner] suggests that the homogeneous unit principle (HUP) espoused by church growth folks at the Fuller School of World Mission is the only way to go in growing a church in the context of ethnic minorities or of any community, for that matter. This principle asserts that churches grow better if the congregants come from the same background (particularly ethnic and socioeconomic).[93]

The homogeneous unit principle is what happens in most congregations in the U.S. When people move into a community, they look around until they

---

92   Felipe Fernández-Armesto, *Near a Thousand Tables: A History of Food* (New York: Free Press, 2002), 167.

93   Ortiz, *One New People*, 45.

find a church that suits them and this, most often, turns out to be a church that has a congregation of people like them. This perpetuates the segregation of congregations in the U.S. Mark DeYmaz writes,

> The problem with the homogeneous unit principle is that despite the good intentions of those interested in rapidly reaching the world with the gospel (and consequently growing churches quickly), the principle has had the unintended effect of justifying the segregation of local congregations along ethnic and economic lines.[94]

HUP comes out of the study of many church congregations, nationally and internationally, and it is a true observation. But I would encourage it to be used with more nuance in its application. I will share more in the following section about how national churches can reach out to immigrant populations.

One challenge to HUP is to ask what kind of growth is being evaluated. Homogeneity may lead to greater numerical numbers, but will it produce the same qualitative growth an interracial, multinational community will produce? The experience of international churches is that the diversity of our communities deepens our faith in Jesus and draws us closer to his world-wide church. Since this works against our natural instinct to seek out others who are like us, worshiping and leading a diverse church community is more difficult. But although difficult, the result is deeper spiritual growth. Stephen Rhodes writes of his experience as pastor of Culmore United Methodist Church, a multiethnic church in Fairfax, Virginia:

> Over the years I have shared stories of Culmore and our international ministry with folks outside our congregation. To my surprise I have received a rather common response. "Oh, that sounds so *interesting*... I'm sure ministry there must be very *challenging*... It must be very *demanding* of you as a pastor."... Being pastor of a multicultural church is interesting, challenging and demanding, but not necessarily in the way that people usually mean. Serving this congregation has been the most exhilarating period of my ministry. Because of the unique demands and challenges, I have grown both as a Christian and as a pastor in ways that might not have been possible in a homogeneous congregation.[95]

---

[94] Mark DeYmaz & Harry Li, *Ethnic Blends: Mixing Diversity into Your Local Church* (Grand Rapids, MI; Zondervan, 2010), 22.

[95] Rhodes, *Where the Nations Meet*, 23.

Mark DeYmaz writes of an experience at a gathering of pastors to interact with a nationally recognized pastor and the author of many books:

> Toward the end of the meeting, an African-American pastor, the leader of a respected multi-ethnic church, entered the room. In spite of the fact that he was somewhat late, and not to mention the only person of color in the room, the meeting's host greeted him warmly, even inviting him to ask the final question. As this pastor would later recall, "There wasn't much time to think, and I hesitated for a moment to ask what was otherwise on my heart. But I went ahead anyway and asked, 'What do you think about the multi-ethnic church?' Without hesitation the speaker bluntly responded, 'I don't recommend it; it's just too difficult. People want to go to church with others who are like them, and I don't think there's anything wrong with that.'"[96]

What is "wrong with that" is that it works against the heart of God for every tribe and every nation to be gathered in worship. Because it is difficult or demanding is not reason to abandon what God calls us to.

A second challenge to the HUP is that our unity in a diverse community is a witness to the world. The world separates into factions; the kingdom of God is drawn to a unity that celebrates its diversity. Ortiz writes of this witness of the multiethnic church:

> Where the context has called us to mirror the gospel of the kingdom in this world of ever increasing diversity, we must take care to be obedient. This is provided by the multiethnic church, a church that reflects the unity of the Godhead, one that introduces the good news to a world that has come to understand hostility and division as the norm.[97]

Congregations that reflect the diversity of the world-wide body of Christ are a witness to the world of the work Jesus came to do and is continuing to do. Stephen Rhodes writes that multicultural congregations are "not God's kingdom come on earth, but they are the foretaste of that kingdom. The way Christians live out God's story in these congregations 'makes the kingdom visible.'"[98]

---

[96] DeYmaz and Li, *Ethnic Blends*, 58–59.

[97] Ortiz, *One New People*, 45.

[98] Rhodes, *Where the Nations Meet*, 223.

Newcomers and visitors to RIC speak with enthusiasm of the joy they experience being part of a community that reflects the diversity of the world. The relationships that cross racial and national lines stand out as exceptional.

A third challenge to the HUP is that God calls us to reach out to the "strangers and aliens" in our midst:

> Leonard Sweet notes that many missiologists have pointed out the theological misnomer of the church's "having a mission": "The church does not have a mission.... It is God who has a mission, and the missionary of God is the Holy Spirit. The question is whether the mission of God has a church."... Will we be bearers of God's universal metanarrative of salvation and blessing to people of all nations, languages and cultures?[99]

So in addition to being a witness to the world, a church that reaches out to the diversity in its neighborhood is being the church God intends it to be. Ortiz spoke with one pastor of a multiethnic church who "shared with me his view that Christians have no option in the matter of evangelism. If the Lord brings to us people of a different culture, we are again faced with the biblical reality that God is no respecter of persons and that we are to serve the world with God's love and compassion."[100]

Will we choose to be obedient to follow Jesus and work with him as he builds his kingdom? Will we allow our communities to define who we are or will we choose to have our identity come from the one we are following? Rhodes writes: "Our congregational diversity includes language, culture, race, class, educational level, theology, and worship style, but the glue that holds all of us together is the theological conviction that our center is Jesus Christ. We are *many* nations, but together we serve *one* Lord."[101]

THREE CHALLENGES FOR NATIONAL CHURCHES FROM INTERNATIONAL CHURCHES

Ken MacHarg recalls that Rev. J.R. "Jack" Collins used to say in the 1970s that international churches are the prototype of what the churches in our home countries should be and will be.[102] This was a prescient observation.

---

[99] Rhodes, 38.

[100] Ortiz, *One New People*, 114.

[101] Rhodes, *Where the Nations Meet*, 13.

[102] Ken MacHarg, email message to author, August 15, 2013.

Because the world has shrunk and the nations of the world are increasingly arriving in the cities and towns of the U.S., international churches need to be studied because what they have experienced over the years is now becoming relevant to churches in the U.S.

International churches are diverse without having to be intentional about it. I like telling people their church can be as wonderful as RIC if they will do two simple things. First, get rid of all English-speaking Protestant churches within an hour and a half drive of your church. Secondly, make sure that no more than 20 percent of your congregation stays for more than ten years.

RIC is a wonderful church because of dynamics forced on us. We would not have chosen to be this way, but having experienced the benefit these dynamics bring, we can see how our international church limitations are a blessing. Churches in the U.S. will have to choose to become more like international churches if they want to reach out to the immigrants of their communities and welcome them as full members.

There are some churches that have reached out to the ethnicities in their neighborhoods. Stephen Rhodes, Manuel Ortiz, and Mark DeYmaz and Harry Li have written books about some of these multiethnic and multicultural churches. When I read their books, I was surprised how similar the dynamics of those churches are to the dynamics of international churches.[103] It is encouraging to read about the ministries of these churches.

One of these churches is Independent Bible Church in Los Angeles with a congregation of Anglos, American Indians, Asian Indians, Blacks, Chinese, Guatemalans, Filipinos, Koreans, Mexicans, Salvadoreans, Russians, Taiwanese, Thais, and Ukrainians. Pastor Mark Oh asks, "How then is a multiethnic church born? It is born in a time of need, situation, and environment in a multiethnic neighborhood. . . . We who live and minister in the inner city neighborhoods cannot avoid multiethnicity today. That is the real America of Los Angeles."[104]

Unfortunately, multiethnic churches are the exception, and the majority of U.S. churches continue to be homogenous congregations—even when other cultures are living in their community. As immigrants move into cities and towns across the U.S., what should the response of churches be? Why should they encourage these immigrants to become a valued part of their church community? What can international churches teach these churches?

---

[103] I used some of their stories to illustrate how the dynamics of international churches affect life and ministry in international churches.

[104] Ortiz, *One New People*, 93.

TAKING ON THE HEART OF JESUS FOR THE WORLD

The first challenge for the national church from the international church is that all followers of Jesus need to take on the heart of Jesus for the world. As we read through Scripture, it is clear that God chooses to love the world:

> The story of Abraham is first and foremost a story about God's mission to the world. God indeed has chosen one nation, but God intends salvation to be available to all. Throughout Scripture God reminds the people of Israel of their sacramental nature: "I am the Lord. . . . I have given you as a covenant to the people, a *light to the nations*, to open the eyes that are blind, to bring out the prisoners from the dungeon" (Is 42:6–7).
>
> "May God be gracious to us and bless us and make his face to shine upon us, that your way may be known upon earth, *your saving power among all the nations*" (Ps 67:1–2).
>
> "To him was given dominion and glory and kingship, *that all peoples, nations, and languages should serve him*" (Dan 7:14).
>
> And in Jesus of Nazareth, descendant of Abraham and Son of God, this mission was reaffirmed: "All authority in heaven and on earth has been given to me. Go therefore and *make disciples of all nations*, baptizing them in the name of the Father and of the Son and of the Holy Spirit" (Mt 28:18–19).[105]

Paul Miller, in his study of the life of Jesus, *Love Walked Among Us*, talks about a pattern in the life of Jesus. Jesus looked, he saw, he had compassion, and then he acted. He illustrates this pattern in several gospel stories; one of these is the story of the blind beggar in John 9. While the disciples turned the blind beggar into a theological question, "Rabbi, who sinned, this man or his parents, that he was born blind?" Jesus looked, saw, had compassion, and acted:

> Analyzing provides the disciples with a safe and tidy world that keeps everything in its place. So they talk to the blind man while they are right in front of him. But Jesus moves toward him, makes mud, and touches his eyes. Jesus lowers himself in order to care, while the disciples elevate themselves in order to judge.
>
> The disciples see a blind man; Jesus sees a man who happens to be blind. The disciples see an item for debate; Jesus sees a person, a

---

[105] Rhodes, *Where the Nations Meet*, 37–38.

human being like himself. They see sin, the effect of man's work; Jesus sees need, the potential for God's work. The disciples see a completed tragedy and wonder who the villain was; Jesus sees a story half-told, with the best yet to come.[106]

When we see immigrants in our communities, what do we see? Do we have God's heart for the world? If the news media and our political discourse is any measure, what we see is disruption to the status quo and a threat to our lifestyle.

The contentious debate about immigration in the U.S. does not reflect God's heart for the world. Rather than see this wave of immigration as an opportunity, too many of those who attend churches in the U.S. see this as a threat. Rhodes writes, "Arguably a land of immigrants, the country today is considerably less hospitable toward international neighbors who are coming to make a home here than it was even a year ago. It is hostility, not hospitality, that most aptly characterizes the current climate of our culture."[107] Defying the biblical admonition to be hospitable, we close our doors and push away the "strangers and aliens" who have become our neighbors.

A root cause of this rejection is found in a projection made in the U.S. 2010 census report:

> With the increasing rise of immigrants in the U.S., the heat of the political battle has increased as politicians seek votes by playing to these fears that the U.S. will be overtaken by foreigners. With 58% of immigrants in the decade 2000–2010 coming from Latin America, the non-Hispanic, white population will be less than half the population of the U.S. in 2043.[108]

This is the fear that is driving the rejection of immigrants, most of whom are coming from non-European countries. Immigrants to the U.S. have always been resisted. It is in our nature to resist change and we fear what these strange immigrants will do to our communities but we forget that the culture we enjoy is the result of the diversity of the immigration that has taken place in the past.

---

[106] Paul Miller, *Love Walked Among Us: Learning to Love Like Jesus* (Colorado Springs, CO: NavPress, 2001), 41.

[107] Rhodes, *Where the Nations Meet*, 15.

[108] "U.S. Census Bureau Projections Show a Slower Growing, Older, More Diverse Nation a Half Century from Now," *United States Census Bureau*, posted December 12, 2012, http://www.census.gov/newsroom/releases/archives/population/cb12-243.html.

Christians can choose to look out at their changing neighborhood, see differences, and fight to protect their culture. It is easy to guard what we have from those we fear will take it away. But how does God see the wave of immigration to the U.S.? When immigrants move into a neighborhood, God sees people he loves, not people who are disturbing the status quo. We hold on to the way things are or the way things used to be; God looks out with expectation to see how his plan will unfold:

> Now should be a time for rejoicing: the Pentecost nature of Christian mission can create new paradigms for witness and evangelization. Instead of rejoicing, we find ourselves threatened and defensive, wondering whether all this heterogeneity is not merely the babblings of a world falling apart, rather than the blessing of a world to which God is giving birth.[109]

The Church in the City in Denver has its beginnings in the work of three men who came each week into the city: one from a Jewish background, one from Nigeria, and the third a Hispanic native to Denver:

> What happened was that we were coming into the city at least three times a week and doing different services out of that church, and what we found was that as we went into these various places, such as shelters, the audience that we were dealing with was very racially mixed. They were either white, Hispanic, American Indian [or] black, and we looked at those sitting out there and realized that there's a common thread that runs through that; it is the need for Christ in their life.[110]

These men looked, saw, had compassion, and acted. They did not see a threat to their identity. They saw people God loves and took on his heart for these people of the inner city. God took their efforts and created a vibrant church that continues to care for the needs of those in the city of Denver.

BECOMING AN INTERNATIONAL CHRISTIAN: THE NEED TO CHANGE OUR IDENTITY

During the Bosnian War (1992–1995), Miroslav Volf, a Croatian, gave a lecture in which he argued that we ought to embrace our enemies as God has embraced us in Christ. Afterwards, Jürgen Moltman asked, "But can you

---

[109] Rhodes, *Where the Nations Meet*, 12.
[110] Ortiz, *One New People*, 55.

embrace a *četnik*?" ("*četniks*" were the Serbian fighters committing horrific crimes against the people of Croatia.)

In response to this question, Volf wrote *Exclusion and Embrace*. Although he wrote this book to explain how the atrocities of the Bosnian War could be understood, what he writes helps us to understand the less violent rejection of immigrants in our communities.

Volf points out that when I create an identity, I automatically create the "other." If my identity is that I am white, then I separate myself from all those who are non-white. If my identity is that I am Presbyterian, then I have separated myself from all those who are not Presbyterian.

The Bosnian War led neighbors who had peacefully coexisted for years to turn against each other in acts of violence when the primary identity in communities changed from being Croatian or Bosnian to being Catholic, Orthodox, or Muslim. In the U.S., this is what leads members of a community to reject the immigrants who arrive. They eat different foods, celebrate different holidays, wear different clothes, and speak a different language. They are strangers and aliens invading our community.

In order to take on the heart of Jesus for the world, our identity must change. Volf says that as followers of Jesus, we must take a step outside our culture. This is the beginning of the path for pilgrims who realize they are aliens to their own culture and have set their hearts on their heavenly home: "At the very core of Christian identity lies an all-encompassing change of loyalty, from a given culture with its gods to the God of all cultures. ... Departure is part and parcel of Christian identity."[111] Through faith one must "depart" from one's culture because the ultimate allegiance is given to God and God's Messiah who transcends every culture.[112]

Like the rulers of Jerusalem who viewed the prophecies of Jeremiah as traitorous utterances, this departure from culture can be threatening. But Jeremiah stayed with the people to whom he prophesied, even when they disobeyed God's Word to them and moved to Egypt. In the same way, we can enjoy our cultural attachments, even while we open ourselves to the cultures of others:

> Christians are not the insiders who have taken flight to a new "Christian culture" and become outsiders to their own culture; rather

---

[111] Miroslav Volf, *Exclusion & Embrace: A Theological Exploration of Identity, Otherness, and Reconciliation* (Nashville, TN, Abingdon, 1996), 40.

[112] Volf, *Exclusion & Embrace*, 49.

when they have responded to the call of the Gospel they have stepped, as it were, with one foot outside their own culture while with the other remaining firmly planted in it. They are distant, and yet they belong.[113]

My identity has changed over the years I have been in an international church. After fifteen years, I am less American and more Christian. I see my culture with different eyes that have the advantage of seeing American culture from a distance. I have learned that Americans are assertive and like tall glasses with lots of ice. And I have learned how powerfully my American identity influences my view of world events.

I was talking with a man from India who had lived in Zimbabwe and defended Robert Mugabe. I was shocked. How could any good person defend a villain who took a prosperous country and devastated its economy with his policies? My friend had an understanding of what colonialism does to a country, as with the British in India, and he understood that in the recovery from colonialism, there will be a measure of further injustice. I never came to agreement with him but I discovered another way of thinking about the issue.

The most disturbing example of my entrenched American identity happened when I heard Loren Cunningham, founder of Youth with a Mission, speak in Rabat. He said that every country has a part of the character of God in it. For example, he said Moroccans have a value of hospitality that is missing in the West. He said that when the Christian population of a country reaches 25 percent, Christian values spill into the culture. He said that every country in the world has smart people and stupid people. But because the population of China is so large, they have a lot more smart people than any other country in the world. And, he continued, when the Christian population of China reached 25 percent, which he expected in the next couple decades, Christian values would spill into the culture of China and China would become the most powerful nation in the world.

My immediate reaction was, "I hope that doesn't happen," and my immediate second reaction was, "Jack, what a jerk you are! You don't want people in China to enter into the kingdom of God so the U.S. can remain the most powerful country in the world?" This is an embarrassing memory because it revealed my nationalism that makes me value nation above Jesus and his kingdom.

---

[113] Volf, *Exclusion & Embrace*, 49.

As I have opened myself to deep relationships with people from other countries and very different backgrounds, I have found myself holding less tightly to my identity as an American. Stephen Rhodes writes, "As Christians, we believe that water is thicker than blood; that our baptism, our connectedness in God, is far more important that the people to whom we are biologically related."[114] This has been my experience in Rabat. Three of my closest friends over the years are men from Ghana, Nigeria, and Ivory Coast. My skin color and nationality give me advantages in the way we are treated in Morocco. Our lives are not the same. We do not have the same benefits. My U.S. passport gives me much greater freedom to travel around the world. There are many differences between us, but what dominates our relationship is that we are followers of God and heading to the same heavenly home. We are eager to work with Jesus as he builds his kingdom. This is what gives our relationship such depth.

Volf writes:

> There is a reality that is more important than the culture to which we belong. It is God and the new world that God is creating, a world in which people from every nation and every tribe, with their cultural goods, will gather around the triune God, a world in which every tear will be wiped away and "pain will be no more" (Revelation 21:3). Christians take a distance from their own culture because they give the ultimate allegiance to God and God's promised future.[115]

I have become less denominational. One of the benefits of living overseas is that I have attended only four Presbytery meetings in my fifteen years and each time I have been shocked at how much the identity of the men and women at the meetings is wrapped up in being Presbyterian. A language is used at these meetings that is foreign to my ears. Political correctness dominates the meeting. As we work through the agenda for the evening, there is a focus on how this denomination that is losing members every year can remain viable. Everything centers around the Presbyterian Church.

I want to stand up and testify to the amazing things God is doing in the world as Jesus builds his kingdom. My identity is that I am a follower of Jesus and that allows me to embrace the wide range of followers of Jesus in the world. If the Presbyterian Church dies, the kingdom of God will move on. I am a follower

---

[114]   Rhodes, *Where the Nations Meet*, 107.
[115]   Volf, *Exclusion & Embrace*, 50–51.

of Jesus, not any particular denomination and this helps me cut through the barriers that separate us.

Rhodes writes,

> As long as Christians continue to divide themselves into groups in order "to make a name," the body of Christ will never be united. As long as we separate ourselves into categories—liberals versus conservatives, evangelicals versus social activists, charismatics versus traditionalists, middle class versus poor, educated versus uneducated, men versus women, white versus nonwhite, American-born versus immigrant—as long as we continue to say, "See how different we are?" we will never be able to accept the radical nature of God's love, which the prophet Joel says God has poured out "on *all flesh*" (Joel 2:28).
>
> Amid our diversity of race, culture, class, gender, language and education, we must realize what we have in common. The only thing that can unite us and make us whole is our salvation in Jesus Christ, God's folly of love revealed in the cross.[116]

When my identity is that I am a follower of God, a child in his family, then I can view immigrants who are followers of Jesus as my brothers and sisters in Christ and be delighted to learn more about my fellow citizens in heaven. And I can view those who are not followers of Jesus as people who Jesus died for, people who Jesus loves. If I have his heart, I will love them in the name of Jesus and allow Jesus to bring new life to them. Volf writes, "The distance from my own culture that results from being born by the Spirit created a fissure in me through which others can come in. The Spirit unlatches the doors of my heart saying: 'You are not only you; others belong to you too.' "[117]

BECOMING GOD'S PEOPLE: BREAKING DOWN BARRIERS

The barriers in the New Testament between Jews and Gentiles were immense and what gave them such strength is that they were created by God. When God gave the Law to Moses, he made it clear that Jews were to be separate from others in the world. Intermarriage was forbidden, as was planting two kinds of seed in the same field or wearing clothing made from wool and linen. This barrier was created by God because he wanted to create a nation of people devoted to him. But at Pentecost God opened the door to the world.

---

[116]　Rhodes, *Where the Nations Meet*, 162.

[117]　Volf, *Exclusion & Embrace*, 51.

Pentecost, the birth of the church, was a breaking down of barriers. The first barrier was the gap between Hebrew and Hellenistic Jews. When the Holy Spirit was poured out on the disciples, they began speaking in other languages, including the languages of the Hellenistic Jews who were visiting Jerusalem for the Feast of Weeks. Peter Wagner writes in his commentary on Acts that there were three parts to Pentecost: Acts 2 in Jerusalem, Acts 8 in Samaria, and Acts 10 in Caesarea.[118]

The Holy Spirit was poured out on those in Jerusalem and the church grew dramatically. The growth of these followers of Jesus began to be a threat and persecution broke out. After Stephen was stoned to death, the followers of Jesus scattered throughout Judea and Samaria. When Phillip preached in Samaria and there was an enthusiastic response, John and Peter came and in a second Pentecost in Acts 8:5–25, the barrier between Jews and Samaritans was broken as the Holy Spirit was poured out on the despised Samaritans. Once again it was Peter at the forefront when God orchestrated his meeting with Cornelius in Acts 10 and now the even more despised Gentiles were brought into the family of God as the Holy Spirit, in a third Pentecost, was poured out on Cornelius and his household.

We are separated from each other by race, politics, national interests, and a seemingly infinite number of other distinctions. This serves the purposes of the devil who seeks to divide and destroy, but it works against the purposes of God who seeks to unite and build.

It is not only those who resist the arrival of immigrants who have biases. Immigrants who come to the U.S. bring with them their own national values and biases. These barriers are broken down when we create relationships and there are followers of Jesus who are reaching out to immigrants, actively welcoming them to the U.S., helping them assimilate to U.S. culture and traditions and make a new start. In the process, immigrants can discover that not all Americans carry guns and not all Americans are sexually promiscuous. The stereotypes they brought with them to the U.S. are challenged as new relationships are forged.

The barriers between immigrants and U.S. citizens do not serve God's purposes and need to be broken down. God wants relationships to be built as people from both sides find their common identity in Jesus. René Padilla exhorts us:

---

[118] C. Peter Wagner, *The Book of Acts* (Grand Rapids, MI: Zondervan, 2001), 71.

Whether a person likes it or not, the same act that reconciles one to God simultaneously introduces the person into a community where people find their identity in Jesus Christ rather than in their race, culture, social class, or sex, and are consequently reconciled to one another. The unifier is Jesus Christ and the unifying principle is the "Gospel."[119]

These three challenges to the national church—discovering the heart of Jesus for the whole world, changing our identity, and breaking down barriers— are what we experience in international church communities.

THREE WAYS NATIONAL CHURCHES CAN BENEFIT FROM THE EXPERIENCE OF INTERNATIONAL CHURCHES

Reading *A Guide to International Church Ministry* will benefit pastors of U.S. congregations that chose to embrace the diversity present in their communities, as well as international church pastors. Let me give three examples.

HOW TO MINISTER TO DIVERSITY

The first is how to have a positive ministry to a diverse congregation. Ministry to a diverse congregation is not easy but it is rewarding. In a sermon to his congregation, Stephen Rhodes preached:

Now I am here to tell you this morning that if it seems more difficult to follow Jesus at Culmore, that's because it is! You have to work harder at it. We do not and will not make it easy or comfortable. There are other churches where everyone is alike: where everyone is of the same race, speaks the same language, has a comparable income, the same educational level, or a similar theological bent. In those churches you can go in and with relative ease find someone who is like you. But at Culmore if you are not willing to go out of your way to intentionally get to know your neighbor, then chances are you won't.[120]

In order for this to work, the choice to reach out to people who are different has to come from the heart. David Packer lists four qualities for international church leadership and among them he says that "leadership must do much more than tolerate difference; they must see them as positive . . . Leadership

---

[119]   C. René Padilla, "The Unity of the Church and the Homogeneous Unit Principle," in *Exploring Church Growth*, ed. Wilbert R. Shenk (Grand Rapids, MI: Eerdmans, 1983), 287.

[120]   Rhodes, *Where the Nations Meet*, 163.

that listens to the concerns and ideas of people from other cultures. We like to be where we are celebrated, not where we are tolerated."[121]

International churches are blessed because diversity is the nature of our communities. But churches in the U.S. must be intentional if they are to minister to a diverse congregation. Both Manuel Ortiz and Stephen Rhodes speak about the intentionality of pastoring a multiethnic church. Ortiz writes: "If we expect [racial tension] to break down by itself without being doggedly intentional about it, we're naive."[122]

What we have discovered in international church ministry is that Wagner is partially correct with his homogenous unity principle. Even in the diversity of an international church, it is necessary to develop programs that minister to the diverse elements of the congregation. What we have learned over the years is that when we try to create programs for the whole of the church, they are not quite successful. We do much better when we create programs for the different segments of the church and then come together to worship on Sunday.

Another way the homogenous unity principle is helpful is with language. When the service must be translated, sermons take twice as long to preach and the quality of the service is diminished. Simultaneous translation works, but this takes talent and it is not always available. Some international churches have headsets so they can hear the translation. It works best when English is a common language and immigrants are encouraged to develop their English skills. Small groups can meet in which the native language is spoken.

Mark Oh, pastor of International Bible Church in Los Angeles, commented, "Unlike some of the bilingual churches which have to translate their services, one of the benefits of the multiethnic church like ours is the use of one common working language—English."[123] This decision was made with the realization that it might exclude some of the recent immigrants.

DeYmaz writes about his understanding of how the homogenous unity principle needs to be selectively applied:

> I believe that the HUP is a valid strategy for evangelism, but a strategy misapplied to the local church. If the goal is to evangelize, then by all means target a people group and provide them with the Word of God in their own language. Sing to them in a musical genre they understand, and become incarnate in their culture so that the gospel

---

[121]   David Packer, *Look Who God Let into the Church*, 13–14.
[122]   Ortiz, *One New People*, 101.
[123]   Ortiz, 93.

is expressed through customs, mores, and traditions they readily embrace. But things change once you commit yourself to establishing a local church. You are no longer at liberty to create a congregation of exclusive worshipers—that's just not a biblical option. According to Paul, the mystery of Christ is "that through the gospel the Gentiles are heirs together with Israel, members together of one body, and sharers together in the promise in Christ Jesus" (Eph. 3:6). Make no mistake: the context in which Paul is writing makes it clear that the "one body" he is talking about is a local church. In other words, "His [Christ's] intent [is] that now, through the church, the manifold wisdom of God should be made known to the rulers and authorities in the heavenly realms" (Eph. 3:10).[124]

FLEXIBILITY IN WORSHIP

A second example of how U.S. churches could learn from international churches has to do with the flexibility in worship we experience. Each year, when new people arrive in the summer and fall, we form new worship teams and these teams bring with them their style of worship. As a result, sometimes our worship has had more of a Pentecostal flavor and at other times, more of an Evangelical flavor. Our current music team has a blend of African-style worship and Caribbean-style worship blended with contemporary worship. I lead once a month and add a bit of liturgy and some traditional hymns. This is part of what makes RIC such a rich church.

The multiethnic churches Ortiz highlights in his book repeatedly spoke of the importance of having this flexibility in worship.

Temple Community Bible Church: "Due to the diversity that exists in this congregation, the pastor leads with an understanding that there are various ways to worship and to remain faithful to the Scriptures. Centeno provides an environment of freedom and assures the members that they may worship, pray, and share in a manner that suits their tradition."[125]

Faith Christian Fellowship: "There is a serious commitment to see the community makeup represented in the church leadership and ministry. There are three styles of worship—gospel from the African-American community, contemporary praise, and classical traditional."[126]

---

[124] DeYmaz and Li, *Ethnic Blends*, 77.

[125] Ortiz, *One New People*, 49.

[126] Ortiz, *One New People*, 52.

The Church in the City: "The worship team is diverse, allowing for music and styles of worship that represent the whole congregation."[127]

When immigrants from the community come to a church, the church can choose to have a style to which they expect people to adapt, or it can value the very rich pool from which it can draw. If a church chooses to keep its style, the church will lose out on the opportunity to celebrate the diversity of cultures that reflect the creativity of God and the immigrant community will be less inclined to stay with this church.

International churches greet each new year with a significantly new congregation. We look around to see who has gifts that can be used to bless the church and then encourage people to use their gifts. National churches can also embrace the diversity of their community. They can build relationships with the ethnic populations in the area of the church. They can get to know their culture, enjoy their food and music, and then encourage some musically talented members of the community to form a worship team that begins to lead in worship once per month. Churches wonder why they are unable to attract ethnic groups to their worship services, but they are unwilling to bend and celebrate the culture of these groups.

FOCUS ON THE CORE OF THE GOSPEL

A third example of how U.S. churches could learn from international churches has to do with a focus on the core of our faith which I discussed in chapter three. Paul wrote in 1 Corinthians, "Jews demand miraculous signs and Greeks look for wisdom, but we preach Christ crucified: a stumbling block to Jews and foolishness to Gentiles, but to those whom God has called, both Jews and Greeks, Christ the power of God and the wisdom of God.[128] And in chapter 2, "When I came to you, brothers, I did not come with eloquence or superior wisdom as I proclaimed to you the testimony about God. For I resolved to know nothing while I was with you except Jesus Christ and him crucified."[129]

It is a focus in our preaching on Christ that unites and builds. This is where life is to be found. Rhodes writes,

> The multicultural church is a constant reminder that spiritual maturity is to be clothed with Christ. The multicultural church understands that it is important to let go of the traditions that have

---

[127] Ortiz, 56.

[128] 1 Corinthians 1:22–24.

[129] 1 Corinthians 2:1-2.

now become stumbling blocks to Christian unity. The multicultural church is willing to hold on to the one tradition that matters—new life in Jesus Christ.[130]

Rhodes spoke with Esther, a leader in the African community, about how the church might reach this community through ministries to single women and their children. Esther replied,

> Pastor, for years I have been helping people with their problems. I listen to them, I pray for them, I help them financially. And sometimes their problems are so big that I feel that my own shoulders will break by helping to carry their burdens. Pastor, I think we should help people with their problems, but that is not where we should begin. You asked me, "What do we have to offer them?" Pastor, just give them Jesus. We can't solve all their problems, but we can point them to the One who can![131]

Sermon series on denominational distinctives help people to become more Methodist, Assemblies of God, or Baptist, but they do not help us to become more Christian. If I preach a sermon series on the baptism of the Holy Spirit or adult baptism by immersion, I unnecessarily divide the church. It is not wrong to take a stand on these issues; it is not wrong to preach sermons about them. But sermons on these peripheral, denominational distinctives should be a small percentage of sermons preached. The dominant themes of preaching should be focused on the core of the gospel.

DeYmaz writes on the importance of protecting the core of faith:

> Of course, in any church, it is important to clarify what you believe. But for those pursuing the multi-ethnic church, it is essential. For with diverse people comes diverse theology; consequently, multi-ethnic church leaders must be up-front and clear about the beliefs of the church in order to "keep the unity of the Spirit through the bond of peace" (Eph. 4:3). We should never compromise our convictions for the sake of diversity. One way to be proactive in this regard is to post a doctrinal statement on your website or in some other visible

---

[130] Rhodes, *Where the Nations Meet*, 45.
[131] Rhodes, 52.

location within the church. I recommend, however, that it speak only about the essential doctrines of the Christian faith, allowing room to accommodate various views on the more nonessential positions of teaching that you will certainly encounter from those seeking to join a multi-ethnic church. Resist the urge to speak to every possible issue in your doctrinal statement, and beyond this, do not be afraid of divergent opinions concerning the nonessentials. As long as those who hold them do not become divisive—by seeking to impose their views on others or by failing to consider others as more important than themselves in the practice of their faith—the healthy dialogue and the exchange of experiential understanding will invite and inspire spiritual growth within the body.[132]

The goal for churches, national or international, is not to become diverse. The goal is not to have a multiethnic church. The goal is to take on Jesus' heart for the world and be obedient to where he calls you.

Let me say that as Christians, we should not pursue racial or cultural diversity simply because it is politically correct (or incorrect, as the case may now be), or because it is the latest theological fad, or even because it is a good conservative or liberal idea. We should do it because it is the gospel. We are called to welcome the world because it is God's mandate for evangelism: "Go therefore and make disciples of *all nations*" (Mt 28:19).[133]

This is the mandate for all followers of Jesus, nationally or internationally. And, as with all of God's commands, when we are obedient, we are blessed. International churches are blessed by the dynamics that shape our existence. As national churches intentionally choose to emulate the circumstances of international churches, they will be blessed as well.

[132] DeYmaz and Li, *Ethnic Blends*, 86–87.
[133] Rhodes, *Where the Nations Meet*, 17.

WHY WE LOVE INTERNATIONAL CHURCHES

Someone has said that leading an international church is like trying to play Bach on a banjo and still make it sound pleasing to the classical musician.[134] Leading an international church is challenging.

David Packer describes the challenges this way:

> Imagine trying to conduct a dramatic play where the actors come and go throughout the presentation. In Scene One the role of "John," for example, is played by an actor named Fred, but by Scene Two Fred has to leave and you need to use Tom. But before Tom gets very far into his part he also has to go and so you use Harry. About this time, however, Harry asks, "Why are we doing this play and not another play?" And, you are not sure how to answer him because frankly, Harry is not a very good "John." The role of "John" has some singing parts and Harry just can't hit the high note.
>
> So you give in and decide to change to another play, one where Harry can hit the high note, and it is okay because about half of the audience has also left and others have come, so they aren't really following the plot all that well anyway—at least not all of them are. Just about the time you get into Act Two of this new play, Harry leaves, but then comes Charlie who really is the perfect "John" of the first play.[135]

International churches are highly transitional and so programming, teaching, preaching, and all other parts of church ministry need to be geared to the short-term. My friend's three-year teaching program did not work in a

[134] Packer, Look *Who God Let into the Church*, 76.
[135] Packer, 53.

church where every year we have a new congregation. When I preached from Romans in the first part of each year for seven years, I had to give a recap of the sermons from the previous year because I knew there were many people who were not at RIC when I last preached from Romans.

When we set out on a program, we need to be flexible and adaptable so we change with the constantly changing needs of the church community. We switch from play to play as Fred, Tom, and Charlie come along and it works out well. But if we become rigid and insist of following a specific program, we are destined for frustration and disillusionment.

Why do we love international churches if there are such difficulties in leading them? The answer is simply that the limiting dynamics of international churches create a wonderful atmosphere for growth in our relationship with Jesus. We rejoice in the diversity of the body of Christ. We delight in the relationships with brothers and sisters from around the world. We look around on Sunday mornings and see a glimpse of what heaven will look like.

Leading an international church may be like playing Bach on a banjo, but there is the inspiration of John King,[136] a Hawaiian who plays Bach on a ukulele that delights trained musical ears. When we persevere, we learn from mistakes and make beautiful music in the international church.

---

[136] "John King Bach Prelude." *YouTube*, https://www.youtube.com/watch?v=935ExOpT5bI.

APPENDIX

Theological Reflections

In *The Sound of Music*, Julie Andrews sings, "Let's start at the very beginning," and that seems good advice. So in talking about international churches we want to know where they began. But before we can talk about the ministry and purpose of international churches, we have to be more clear about the theological underpinnings of international churches. In many ways the theology that undergirds an international church is no different from that of a national church, but the dynamics of international churches allow these theological underpinnings to be experienced more vibrantly. In this chapter I will discuss ten of them.

First is the Trinity. This is where every part of Christian faith begins. If we want to understand what we believe, we have to start at the very beginning, before the beginning of this world. When we have a better understand of the relationships of Father, Son, and Holy Spirit, we can begin to understand who we are and what we are expected to do.

Second is community. Because the Triune God created us to be in fellowship with Father, Son, and Holy Spirit, we are created to be in community. Why do we seek out other followers of Jesus wherever we go? Because we are created to live in community.

Third is unity. In our community we are to seek unity. As the Father, Son, and Holy Spirit are unified, so are we to live united in community. Unfortunately, our unity is shattered by our sinful human nature and diverse theologies. We divide what God wants to be unified. We create human institutions that do not recognize the validity of other institutions.

Fourth is diversity. Unity does not mean conformity. Unity does not need to create homogeneity. We are created by God who loves diversity and so we celebrate our diversity even as we focus on the core of our faith.

Fifth is the translation of the gospel. The diversity of the worldwide church is not only celebrated, it is essential if the gospel is to pass on to new generations and new cultures. The survival of the church depends on the gospel being continually retranslated.

Sixth, while the diversity of the church may be necessary and celebrated, it creates tensions in the church, and so in order to seek unity in our diversity, we have to examine what is the core of our faith around which we can find unity.

Seventh, because culture attaches itself to the gospel, in order to have a clear view of the core of our faith, disenculturation must be addressed.

Eighth is the understanding that we are on pilgrimage, heading toward our heavenly home. This world is not our home. We keep our sights on our heavenly home. As we are on pilgrimage to our heavenly home, we do best when we live in the present, grateful for the past, but moving into the future.

Ninth is our perspective that we are aliens living in a strange land. We realize that this world is not our home and that we are simply passing through the few, short years of our earthly existence.

Tenth is the realization that because we are aliens on pilgrimage to our eternal home, we live in the present. We are not stuck in the past because we do not have a past. We live in the present with our eyes fixed on what God will be doing in our midst.

TRINITY

The doctrine of the Trinity is sometimes viewed like the slightly crazy uncle who shows up at a family reunion. You hope that he will stay in a corner somewhere and not attract attention. When someone tries to explain the Trinity, they are forced to revert to imperfect analogies. There are the three forms of water: ice, water, and steam. There is the egg: shell, yolk, and egg white. But whatever the analogy, it leads to one heresy or another.[137] It seems impossible for three persons to be one God. That is the problem. You can have one man with three roles, father, husband, and employee, but that is not three persons.

Michael Reeves, in his book, *Delighting in the Trinity*, affirms this discomfort many Christians have with the doctrine of the Trinity:

> Whether the Trinity is compared to shrubbery, streaky bacon, the three states of H_2O or a three-headed giant, it begins to sound, well, bizarre, like some pointless and unsightly growth on our

---

[137] For a delightful satire of Trinity analogies, see Hans Fiene, "The Lutheran Satire," http://www.youtube.com/watch?v=KQLfgaUoQCw.

understanding of God, one that could surely be lopped off with no consequence other than a universal sigh of relief.[138]

Because every analogy for the Trinity is inadequate and unsatisfying, for the forty years of my life as a follower of Jesus I avoided this doctrine as much as possible. Living in a country that is 99 percent Muslim made this especially convenient since the doctrine of the Trinity is one of the points of attack against Christian faith.

But then, as a result of the insights of Ellis Potter, Lesslie Newbigin, and Michael Reeves, I learned to put the doctrine of the Trinity at the center of all my understanding of theology and Christian life. I pulled the uncle out of the corner and made him the honored guest. The consequence is that I have a deeper, more solid basis for what I believe. I am not alone in my treatment of the doctrine of the Trinity. Lesslie Newbigin writes,

> [The Trinity] has been treated like the talent that was buried for safekeeping rather than risked in the commerce of discussion. The church continues to repeat the Trinitarian formula but—unless I am greatly mistaken—the ordinary Christian in the Western world who hears or reads the word "God" does not immediately and inevitably think of the Triune Being—Father, Son, and Spirit. He thinks of a supreme monad.[139]

Ellis Potter, former pastor of the Basel Christian Fellowship and a former member of L'Abri Fellowship, has written a book titled *3 Theories of Everything*. In it he discusses three absolutes, three world views: Monism, Dualism, and Trinitarianism. Monism is not monotheism. Monism is "the belief in one One, a total unity that is the ground of everything."[140] This is the world view of Hinduism and Buddhism. And, Potter says, this is also the world view of Islam in which "Allah is one. There is no other. He has no son. There is a very strong unity and absoluteness in Allah. He is not intrinsically relational. If Allah wants to talk to somebody and function as a personal god, then he has to create somebody to talk to."[141]

---

[138]   Michael Reeves, *Delighting in the Trinity: An Introduction to the Christian Faith* (Downers Grove, IL: IVP, 2012), 10.

[139]   Lesslie Newbigin, *The Open Secret: An Introduction to the Theology of Mission* (Grand Rapids, MI: Eerdmans, 1995), 27.

[140]   Ellis Potter, *3 Theories of Everything* (n.p.: Destinée Media, 2013), 9.

[141]   Potter, *3 Theories of Everything*, 87.

Dualism is the world view of Taoism and Confucianism. In Korea the circle of Dualism is known as the *umyang*. In China it is the *yin* and *yang* that is more familiar to the West. "Yin means dark and yang means light, and they symbolize the idea that absolute reality consists of opposites in harmony.... The idea behind Dualism is that life is good when opposites are in proper balance, or are in harmony with each other, but we suffer when there is imbalance or disharmony."[142]

Trinitarianism observes the world and sees unity and diversity. But whereas Monism sees unity as good and diversity as bad, Trinitarianism regards "the original perfection, which is called God, as both perfectly unified and perfectly diversified ... God is perfectly unified as one God, and yet God is perfectly diversified in the three persons of the Father, Son, and Holy Spirit. There is unity and diversity in absolute reality."[143]

God is a personal God. Followers of Jesus distinguish between the religion of Christianity and having a personal relationship with God through Jesus Christ. As Potter puts it, "God was a personal God before I was born. That He is personal is completely independent of creation, and stems from there being three persons in relationship with each other."[144]

The Triune God existed in relationship for an eternity before the universe was created. In this relationship, the Triune God has needs that are perfectly met within the relationships of the Trinity. Potter points out that we have needs to be seen, to be heard, to make a difference, and to be wanted.[145] We want to be recognized, respected, and honored. We want to belong, to be affirmed, and to be valued. These are not signs of weakness. These are not human frailties. We are created with these needs because we are created in the image of God who has these same needs. The difference between our needs and the needs of our creator is that the needs of the Father, Son, and Holy Spirit are perfectly met within the relationships of the Trinity while we are created with needs that are unmet without a relationship with Jesus. God does not need us but we need God. God wants us but does not need us.

> Why do we have these needs? ... According to the third circle, human beings are made in God's image. Their needs come from God because God has those needs.... It's not that God needs anything from

---

[142] Potter, 29.

[143] Potter, 38.

[144] Potter, 53.

[145] Potter, 58–59.

us. Rather, He has needs among Himself, and exactly the same needs we have—to be seen, to be heard, to make a difference, and to be wanted. But God does not suffer from these needs. Having these needs is pure joy for God, because needs are the basis for trust and love. A need that can only be fulfilled by another person requires that you trust that person to fulfill it. If there were no needs, there would be no real trust or love.... Each of the three persons of God fills the needs of the other persons, and does so by emptying Himself for the others. Jesus empties Himself for the Father and the Holy Spirit. For this reason, the center of reality for Jesus is not in Jesus, it's in the Father and Holy Spirit. Each of the persons of God is similarly other-centered rather than centered in Himself. Such is the Bible's depiction of absolute reality: a totally other-centered God. This other-centeredness is the source of God's energy, for as each of the person of God empties Himself once, He is filled twice by the others.... The Bible gives a name to this energy when it says *God is love.*[146]

The understanding that "God is love" rests in the relationships of the Trinity is not just a recent understanding of the church. Richard of St. Victor was a prominent mystical theologian and prior of the famous Augustinian Abbey of Saint Victor in Paris from 1162 until his death in 1173. Reeves shares Richard's insights about the nature of God as a God of love, "Richard argued that if God were just one person, he could not be intrinsically loving, since for all eternity (before creation) he would have had nobody to love."[147]

Reeves asks the question: What was God doing before creation? And his answer is that before creation the Triune God existed in relationships of love. "Jesus tells us explicitly in John 17:24. 'Father,' he says, 'you loved me before the creation of the world.' And that is the God revealed by Jesus Christ. Before he ever created, before he ever ruled the world, before anything else, this God was a Father loving his Son."[148]

"God is, before all things, a Father ... He is Father. All the way down. Thus all that he does he does as Father. That is who he is. He creates as a Father and he rules as a Father."[149] "The Son is the *eternal* Son. There was never a time when he didn't exist."[150]

---

[146] Potter, *3 Theories of Everything*, 59–60.
[147] Reeves, *Delighting in the Trinity*, 31.
[148] Reeves, *Delighting in the Trinity*, 21.
[149] Reeves, 23.
[150] Reeves, 27.

There is a very definite shape to their relationship. Overall, the Father is the lover, the Son is the beloved. The Bible is awash with talk of the Father's love for the Son, but while the Son clearly loves the Father, hardly anything is said about it. The Father's love is primary. The Father is the loving head. That then means that in his love he will send and direct the Son, whereas the Son never sends or directs the Father.[151]

"The Spirit stirs up the delight of the Father in the Son and the delight of the Son in the Father, inflaming their love and so binding them together in 'the fellowship of the Holy Spirit' (2 Cor 13:14)."[152] Father, Son, and Holy Spirit existed for an eternity before the creation of the universe in a harmony of love and unity. When the Trinity is the starting point, then it becomes clear why we need community, why international churches exist.

The Trinity has an outward, other-oriented focus and so the universe was created and mankind was created in the image of God. The Triune God wanted to share its fellowship with others and so, from the beginning, the desire was for men and women to be brought into relationship with the Triune God.

But in order to do this, it was necessary for man to have free will. It was necessary that man choose to be in relationship with the Triune God. With the gift of free will came the possibility of choosing against a relationship with the Triune God and so sin entered the world. God did not create evil, but "by graciously giving his creatures the room to exist, the Triune God allows them the freedom to turn away without himself being the author of evil."[153]

This sin created distance between God and ourselves, so God had to act. Left to ourselves we would be lost. But because God so much desired us to be in relationship with himself, God incarnated himself (Jesus), to live among us, to show us who God is, to die in our place. He paid the penalty of death for our sins and broke the power of death. He resurrected, giving us hope of eternal life when we die our physical death. Jesus ascended into heaven and the Holy Spirit came to work in us and prepare us for the time when we will all be brought into heaven.

The Trinity is the beginning and ending point of all theology and we offer ourselves to the Triune God in grateful praise as in this Trinitarian prayer of John Stott:

---

[151]   Reeves, 28.

[152]   Reeves, 29.

[153]   Reeves, 58.

Good morning heavenly Father,
good morning Lord Jesus,
good morning Holy Spirit.

Heavenly Father, I worship you as the creator and sustainer of the universe.
Lord Jesus, I worship you, Savior and Lord of the world.
Holy Spirit, I worship you, sanctifier of the people of God.

Glory to the Father, and to the Son and to the Holy Spirit.

Heavenly Father, I pray that I may live this day in your presence and please you more and more.

Lord Jesus, I pray that this day I may take up my cross and follow you.

Holy Spirit, I pray that this day you will fill me with yourself and cause your fruit to ripen in my life: love, joy, peace, patience, kindness, goodness, faithfulness, gentleness and self-control.

Holy, blessed and glorious Trinity, three persons in one God, have mercy upon me. Amen.

COMMUNITY

The core of our Christian faith, the Trinity and the Incarnation, provide an understanding of why followers of Jesus meet in community rather than sit in their homes as individuals. Because God exists in community, we are also created to live in community.

What kind of community should we be? Should we try to be like the early Palestinian church? Is that our model? Andrew Walls points out in *The Missionary Movement in Christian History*:

At the heart of Jewish faith, as at the heart of Islamic faith, is the Prophetic Word—God speaks to humanity. At the heart of Christian faith is the Incarnate Word—God became human. The divine Word was expressed under the conditions of a particular human society; the divine Word was, as it were, *translated*. And since the divine Word is for all humanity, he is translated again in terms of every culture where he finds acceptance among its people. The unchanging nature of the Prophetic Word of the Qur'an, fixed in heaven forever in Arabic, produces a single Islamic civilization recognizable, despite all the local variations, from Indonesia to Morocco. There can be no single Christian civilization.... Christian faith, then, rests on a massive divine act of translation, and proceeds by successive lesser acts of translation into the complexes of experiences and relationships that form our social identities in different parts of the world auditorium.[154]

This means that the goal of the church is not to emulate the early Palestinian church; the goal is to emulate the Trinity. In the way that the Trinity honors each person of the Trinity, deflects glory to the other persons of the Trinity, and values the other persons of the Trinity, so are we to honor each other, value each other, and serve each other in our Christian communities.

Paul's encouragement to the Philippians to imitate Christ lists behaviors that are found in the Trinity:

> If you have any encouragement from being united with Christ, if any comfort from his love, if any fellowship with the Spirit, if any tenderness and compassion, then make my joy complete by being like-minded, having the same love, being one in spirit and purpose. Do nothing out of selfish ambition or vain conceit, but in humility consider others better than yourselves. Each of you should look not only to your own interests, but also to the interests of others.[155]

This is the ideal, but which of the New Testament churches modeled these behaviors for us? In the early church in Jerusalem there was tension because the Greek-speaking Jews thought the distribution to widows was unequal and unfair. The church in Corinth divided into factions. The early church that had the first, Jewish, believers tried to impose their Jewish traditions on the Gentile followers of Jesus. Paul is not urging us to be like any of these churches. He is urging us to be like the Triune God, and like the Triune God we are meant to live in community.

Lesslie Newbigin makes this point in *The Gospel in a Pluralistic Society*:

> From the very beginning the Bible sees human life in terms of relationships.... Human life is seen in terms of mutual relationships ... man and woman ... parents and children ... families and clans and

[154] Andrew Walls, *The Missionary Movement in Christian History: Studies in the Transmission of Faith* (Maryknoll, NY: Orbis Books, 1996), 47.
[155] Philippians 2:1–4.

nations. The Bible does not speak about "humanity" but about "all the families of the earth" or "all the nations."

There is, there can be, no private salvation, no salvation which does not involve us with one another. . . . God's saving revelation of himself does not come to us straight down from above—through the skylight, as we might say it. In order to receive God's saving revelation we have to open the door to the neighbor whom he sends as his appointed messenger. . . . There is no salvation except one in which we are saved together through the one whom God sends to be the bearer of his salvation.[156]

We are saved into relationship with the Triune God and into relationship with each other. Why is it incorrect to say, "I am a Christian but I don't like the church so I commune with God in nature?" It is because we were saved into a community of relationships with others made in the image of God, not to commune with squirrels and rabbits. As pleasant as that might be, it is not a substitute for community.

We have a community identity. As Peter writes,

But you are a chosen people, a royal priesthood, a holy nation, God's special possession, that you may declare the praises of him who called you out of darkness into his wonderful light. Once you were not a people, but now you are the people of God; once you had not received mercy, but now you have received mercy.[157]

It is out of our community that the gospel flows. It is our life in community that God uses to proclaim his truth. How does the world know what we say about Jesus is true? Jesus told his disciples, "By this everyone will know that you are my disciples, if you love one another."[158]

In Jesus' high priestly prayer recorded in John 17, he prays:

I do not ask for these only, but also for those who will believe in me through their word, that they may all be one, just as you, Father, are in me, and I in you, that they also may be in us, so that the world may believe that you have sent me. The glory that you have given me I

---

[156] Lesslie Newbigin, *The Gospel in a Pluralist Society* (Grand Rapids, MI: Eerdmans, 1989), 82.
[157] 1 Peter 2:9–10 (NIV).
[158] John 13:35 (NIV).

have given to them, that they may be one even as we are one, I in them and you in me, that they may become perfectly one, so that the world may know that you sent me and loved them even as you loved me.[159]

Our community is our witness. Lesslie Newbigin points out that the preaching of the disciples, when the twelve were sent out, followed their acts of healing, "Almost all of the great Christian preachings in Acts are made in response to a question. Something has happened which makes people aware of a new reality, and therefore the question arises: What is this reality? The communication of the gospel is the answering of that question."[160] When we live and love and give praise to God in community, questions are raised that then can be answered. It is out of our relationships that the gospel comes to the world.

Even our going out into the world with the gospel comes (or at least should come) out of a desire to be in relationship:

> "Where I am, there shall my servant be" (John 12:26). The one who has been called and loved by the Lord, the one who wishes to love and serve the Lord, will want to be where he is. . . . At the heart of mission is simply the desire to be with him and to give him the service of our lives. At the heart of mission is thanksgiving and praise. . . . Mission is an acted out doxology. That is its deepest secret. Its purpose is that God may be glorified.[161] Why did Peter ask Jesus, "If it is you, tell me to come to you on the water?"[162]

Peter had a desire to be with Jesus, to do with Jesus the things he did. He had learned when the twelve were sent out that Jesus had given them the power to do the impossible things he did. So when he saw Jesus, he knew that if this apparition really was Jesus, he would be able to walk out and be with him.

Our proper motivation to go out into the world with the gospel is not to be obedient but to be where Jesus is. Reeves makes this point:

> The truth is that God is *already* on mission: in love, the Father has sent his Son and his Spirit. It is the outworking of his very nature . . . when Jesus sends us, he is allowing us to *share* the missional, generous, outgoing shape of God's own life. . . . Jesus is found *out there*, in the

---

159 John 17:20–23 (ESV).
160 Newbigin, *The Gospel in a Pluralist Society*, 132.
161 Newbigin, 127.
162 Matthew 14:28.

place of rejection. That is where the Father has sent him, that he might bring sinners back as children. The Christian life is one of being where he is, of joining in how he has been sent.[163]

Jesus is working to save this generation. When people in the Muslim world have dreams of a man in white who weeps with them for the sorrows in their lives, who is it they dream of? It is Jesus.[164]

If we want to be with Jesus, then we need to go out into our neighborhood, workplace, and the world to share the gospel. This is the work of Jesus and it is our privilege to be able to share with him in his work.

God's relational desire for us explains why we have sacraments in the church. A man from Southeast Asia made the decision to convert from Islam to following Jesus. He asked me about baptism and why it was necessary. I explained that Catholics believe baptism is necessary for salvation but that Protestants believe it is a public declaration of a private decision to follow Jesus. I said that this is best understood when we see that God wants us to live in relationship. This is why we make public what we privately decide.

This is also why we celebrate communion together. This is a meal in which we, together, remember what Jesus has done for us and, together, look forward to the meal we will share with Jesus when we come into his kingdom.

Some people, when they go overseas, take a break from church. For them, Sunday morning is a morning to sleep in, relax, and maybe play some golf. Weekends are also a good time to explore this foreign land; it seems a waste not to take advantage of the two to four years they are there.

Others stay away from church because they don't want to take the trouble to go to an unfamiliar church with a different worship style, different style of preaching, and people not like them when they will leave in a few years anyway. But RIC and other international churches exist because we are created to live in community that loves and serves each other as Father, Son, and Holy Spirit do in the Trinity. There is nothing distinctive about international churches in this regard. All followers of Jesus have this same need. Wherever we are, we need to seek out fellowship to be encouraged to follow Jesus and to give him praise.

UNITY

The Triune God—Father, Son, and Holy Spirit—existed in eternity before the creation of the universe in a relationship that is so perfect that there is one

---

[163]   Reeves, *Delighting in the Trinity*, 105–106.
[164]   Tom Doyle and Greg Webster, *Dreams and Visions: Is Jesus Awakening the Muslim World?* (Nashville, TN: Nelson, 2012).

God. And since we have been created by the other-centered Triune God that wanted us to share in their fellowship, we are to be like the Triune God in a community that is so unified that we are one people.

Unity has been a driving force throughout biblical history and explains God's reaction to all the conflict among his chosen people. The strongest condemnations of the prophets are reserved for Israel and Judah who fought a 300-year civil war. By comparison, Egypt and Assyria, and Babylon get off easy. This war between God's chosen people, Judah and Israel, was what was most disturbing to God.

The teaching of divorce, that what God has united should not be separated,[165] is another example of God's concern for unity among his chosen people. And in Matthew 18, Jesus taught about how to discipline a brother or sister who sins. The process is meant to bring to repentance and to maintain unity in the body. The center of Jesus' high priestly prayer in John 17 is concerned with unity, "All I have is yours, and all you have is mine. And glory has come to me through them. I will remain in the world no longer, but they are still in the world, and I am coming to you. Holy Father, protect them by the power of your name—the name you gave me—so that they may be one as we are one."[166]

Unity is so vital that one of the first issues Paul dealt with in his first letter to the church in Corinth was divisions among the church:

> Brothers, I could not address you as spiritual but as worldly— mere infants in Christ. I gave you milk, not solid food, for you were not yet ready for it. Indeed, you are still not ready. You are still worldly. For since there is jealousy and quarreling among you, are you not worldly? Are you not acting like mere men? For when one says, "I follow Paul," and another, "I follow Apollos," are you not mere men?[167]

It is because of his concern for unity that Paul was so upset with the Corinthians who were taking each other to court:

> The very fact that you have lawsuits among you means you have been completely defeated already. Why not rather be wronged? Why not rather be cheated? Instead, you yourselves cheat and do wrong, and you do this to your brothers.[168]

---

165 Matthew 19:6.
166 John 17:10–11.
167 1 Corinthians 3:1–4.
168 1 Corinthians 6:7–8.

The list of behaviors God opposes in the New Testament are opposed, in part, because they work against unity. Quarreling, jealousy, outbursts of anger, factions, slander, gossip, arrogance, and disorder all break relationships, creating disunity in a church community. These behaviors are not only harmful to the individual but to the whole community.

Unfortunately, the history of the church is a history of division and separation. Martin Luther was cut off from the Roman Catholic Church and now church splits are so common they are a subject for satire as in this *Tom in the Box* report: "Forty-Seven Church Splits Finally Brings Doctrinal Perfection." This report gives the history of a church that split forty-seven times and ended up being called: "The Presbyterian Totally Reformed Covenantal Westminsterian Sabbatarian Regulative Credo-Communionist Amillennial Presuppositional Church of Centerville" or PTRCWSRCCAPCC. They have six members but hope to grow.[169]

As I mentioned in the section on the Trinity, unity does not mean conformity. God delights in diversity. This is true of the created world and it is true of cultures, languages, and even denominations. Jeremiah Burroughs, a seventeenth-century Puritan, was a leading spokesman for the "Independents" who resisted the control of the Catholics, Anglicans, or any other religious group. Bruce Guenther lists six principles distilled from the writings of Burroughs[170] that reveal a healthy view of denominations and other strains in the worldwide body of Christ:

> First, doctrinal differences among Christians are inevitable. "So long as we live here in this muddy world," writes Burroughs, there will continue to be divisions even among godly truth-seeking persons, particularly on secondary matters. Burroughs readily acknowledged that some divisions among Christians are due to human weakness and sin, but there are some matters on which the Bible is simply not clear. The reality of differences does not, however, give license to condemn others as false or as apostate; rather, it requires a posture of humility on the part of all Christians as they recognize the limitations of their own understanding.
>
> Second, doctrinal differences in secondary matters are still important. Burroughs argues that only the Bible, and not any human

---

[169] Thomas Slawson, "Forty-Seven Church Splits Finally Brings Doctrinal Perfection," *Tom in the Box*, http://www.tominthebox.net/2008/01/forty-seven-church-splits-finally.html.
[170] Distilled by the American historian, Winthrop Hudson.

authority, has the right to dictate to the conscience its understanding on secondary matters. Christians are obligated to practice what they believe and to pursue the implications of honestly held convictions. Denominations are a place where differences can manifest themselves without creating intense conflict among Christians.

Third, differences among Christians can be useful. Burroughs argues that even divisions precipitated by human weakness and sin can be used by God for his own purposes.

Fourth, because no group of Christians has a complete grasp of divine truth, the true Church of Christ can never be fully represented by any single ecclesiastical structure. Burroughs and his colleagues argued that the New Testament had not prescribed one particular way of organizing Christian communities.

Fifth, true unity among Christians is based on the common gospel and overshadows other differences that may exist among Christians. True unity should be expressed through cooperation between denominations. Burroughs makes it very clear that all Christians, despite their differences, are nevertheless united in Christ.

Sixth, denominational diversity is not necessarily schism. The problem of what to do when an institutional expression of the church becomes corrupt or apostate has often created dilemmas for Christians. The fact that alternative denominational options exist has made it possible for some Christians to live an authentic life of discipleship and witness to the gospel of Jesus Christ (e.g., the confessing church in Germany during the 1930s). As Hans Küng has pointed out, in such instances, it is not denominationalism that is the cause of disunity, but rather careless syncretism.[171]

At a time when denominations were being created, Burroughs saw the benefit of denominations. There is beauty in diversity and God delights in diversity. Some followers of Jesus prefer more mystery and nuance, others prefer a more black and white theology. Rich Mullins, best known for his song, "Our God Is an Awesome God," was very catholic in his love of the church. He said in one of his concerts,

I have a huge respect for the Quakers as people. My only hang-up with it right now is that it's so watered down. I mean, they're just like Nazarenes that don't baptize. I always wished they'd be more "Quakerly." But I wish that about everyone. I wish Baptists would be more Baptist, and I wish Anglicans would be more Anglican. We don't all have to agree. You know, a lot of people think that the idea that there's so many denominations is disillusioning. And I just kind of go, I'm glad the Baptists can go to their own place to worship, because I'm not sure I want to do it the way they do it.[172]

It is not denominations per se that are problematic, but the polity of denominations that divides us: not recognizing each other as brothers and sisters in Christ and not permitting us to assemble together to share the Lord's Supper. Those who create and perpetuate these divisions should be trembling in their shoes as they await God's judgment for dividing the family of God.

Once again, this is where international churches shine. We discover unity in the midst of a diverse community. God works to build, create, unite. The Devil works to destroy, kill, and divide. In an international church we are working with God to bring unity to the diverse community he is creating.

DIVERSITY

As with all of our theology, the importance of diversity begins with the Trinity. Father, Son, and Holy Spirit existed for eternity, in a fellowship so unified we worship one God. The God we worship is perfectly diversified and perfectly unified.[173] The world sees diversity and unity as antithetical, but the Triune God brings diversity and unity together and this is the model for the community God has called together to worship and serve him.

God's love of diversity is seen in his answer to Job and his friends' questions about the presence of suffering and evil in this world. For thirty-seven chapters Job and his friends gave opinions and asked questions about why Job had suffered so much, and when God finally spoke to Job he did so with a nature documentary in which his delight with the diversity of his creation is evident:

> Where were you when I laid the earth's foundation?
> Tell me, if you understand.

---

[172] James Bryan Smith, *Rich Mullins: A Devotional Biography, An Arrow Pointing to Heaven* (Nashville, TN: Broadman, 2002), 49–50.

[173] Potter, *3 Theories of Everything*, 37.

Do you hunt the prey for the lioness
and satisfy the hunger of the lions
when they crouch in their dens
or lie in wait in a thicket?
Who provides food for the raven
when its young cry out to God
and wander about for lack of food?
Do you know when the mountain goats give birth?
Do you watch when the doe bears her fawn?
Who let the wild donkey go free?
Who untied his ropes?
Will the wild ox consent to serve you?
Will he stay by your manger at night?
The wings of the ostrich flap joyfully,
but they cannot compare with the pinions and feathers of the stork.
Do you give the horse his strength
or clothe his neck with a flowing mane?
Does the hawk take flight by your wisdom
and spread his wings toward the south?
Does the eagle soar at your command
and build his nest on high?[174]

God's love of his diverse creation is also seen in the opening chapters of the Bible. In the Genesis story of creation God creates and then makes his judgment about what he has created. At the end of each day, God viewed his work and pronounced it as being good. On day three he created plants and trees of various kinds. *And God saw that it was good.* On day five he created the creatures of the sea and the birds of the air. *And God saw that it was good.* On day six he created animals for the land. *And God saw that it was good.*

Genesis does not go into detail about the kinds of plants and animals he created but the incredible beauty and diversity of what he created is portrayed in the BBC series *Planet Earth,* which uses amazing photography to show life in forests, the sea, deserts, caves, in all corners of the earth.[175] *Planet Earth* is a video presentation of Job 38–41 and after watching the episodes, all one can do is sit back in amazement at the creatively beautiful work of God. God created,

---

[174] Job 38:4, 39–41, 39:1, 5, 9, 13.
[175] *Planet Earth,* directed by Alastair Fothergill, aired March 25, 2007 (BBC Video, 2007).

sat back to evaluate his diverse creation, and pronounced it as good. God was satisfied, pleased with his creation.

On the sixth day God created man and woman in his image. This was again a creation of diversity. Male and female he made them.[176] But he created them to be "one flesh."[177] In this we see how we are to model the Trinity. We are to be diverse and yet unified.

Reeves comes to the same conclusion and makes a great distinction between oneness and sameness:

> Oneness for the single-person God would mean *sameness*. Alone for eternity without any beside him, why would he value others and their differences? Think how it works out for Allah: under his influence, the once-diverse cultures of Nigeria, Persia, and Indonesia are made, deliberately and increasingly, *the same.* Islam presents a complete way of life for individuals, nations and cultures, binding them into one way of praying, one way of marrying, buying, fighting, relating—even, some would say, one way of eating and dressing.
>
> Oneness for the triune God means *unity*. As the Father is absolutely one with his Son, and yet is not his Son, so Jesus prays that believers might be one, but not that they might all be the same. Created male *and* female, in the image of this God, and with many other good differences between us, we come together valuing the way the triune God has made us each unique.[178]

The story of the Tower of Babel[179] offers an explanation for how there came to be so many nations speaking so many languages and is an indictment of our human desire to control and manage God.[180] But it is not a condemnation of our diversity. Though I often regret the linguistic barriers that complicate relationships with others in the world, the diversity of languages and cultures is not God's punishment. The story of the Tower of Babel is about our desire to control and language is incidental to the story.

Stephen Rhodes presents a defense for the blessing of languages in his book and concludes, "Seen in this context, linguistic, familial, and national diversity

---

[176] Genesis 1:27.

[177] Genesis 2:24.

[178] Reeves, *Delighting in the Trinity*, 104.

[179] Genesis 11:1–9.

[180] John Walton, *Genesis*, NIVAC (Grand Rapids, MI: Zondervan, 2001), 377.

are not curses of divine wrath but fulfillment of the blessing of creation. A multilingual and multinational humanity was God's intention all along."[181]

I have observed families where the members are fluent in Arabic, French, and English. As the conversation proceeds, they switch easily from one language to another. I ask why they do this and they say that some things are better communicated in one language than another. If we are fluent in the languages of the world in heaven, this would make for some stimulating conversations.

Stanley Hauerwas writes, "God's confusing the people's language as well as his scattering of them was meant as a gift. For by being so divided, by having to face the otherness crated by separateness of language and place, people were given the resources necessary to recognize their status as creatures."[182]

In Acts 17, Paul stated in his Aeropagus address that God created the nations of men, "From one man he made every nation of men, that they should inhabit the whole earth; and he determined the times set for them and the exact places where they should live."[183]

The diverse ethnic groups in the world are loved and pursued by Jesus to draw them into his kingdom. In Revelation 5 after the Lamb opened the scroll and seven seals, the heavenly creatures sang a new song:

> You are worthy to take the scroll and to open its seals, because you were slain, and with your blood you purchased men for God from every tribe and language and people and nation. You have made them to be a kingdom and priests to serve our God, and they will reign on the earth.[184]

And then in Revelation 7 the great multitude of those who have been redeemed by God gave praise:

> After this I looked and there before me was a great multitude that no one could count, from every nation, tribe, people and language, standing before the throne and in front of the Lamb. They were wearing white robes and were holding palm branches in their hands. And they cried out in a loud voice: "Salvation belongs to our God, who sits on the throne, and to the Lamb."[185]

---

[181] Stephen A. Rhodes, *Where the Nations Meet: The Church in a Multicultural World* (Downers Grove, IL: IVP, 2012), 24.

[182] Stanley Hauerwas, *Christian Existence Today: Essays on Church, World and Living in Between* (Durham, NC: Labyrinth, 1988), 49.

[183] Acts 17:26–27.

[184] Revelation 5:9–10.

[185] Revelation 7:9–10.

God calls us to unity but not at the expense of our diversity. Diversity is valued by God and should be valued by us, but diversity can never be valued at the expense of holiness and righteousness. When diversity becomes our primary focus, it becomes a false idol and we are pulled away from our devotion to God. This is seen most clearly in many mainline denominations who seem to have replaced the Holy Trinity of Father, Son, and Holy Spirit with the unholy trinity of diversity, tolerance, and inclusion. PCUSA, the denomination I belong to, has a Committee on Representation[186] that regulates the inclusiveness and diversity of church councils. I understand the value of this, but the intention seems to be that if we focus on being diverse, we will become diverse. This is like stroking the leaves of a plant rather than feeding its roots with water and nutrients. Authentic diversity results from a focus on Jesus. Because God loves the world and not just any one particular part of the world, when we focus on him, lift praise to him in worship, and try to become more like Christ, our hearts will be opened to all the world, not just the part most like us.

When people from mainline denominations visit our international church in Rabat, they are stunned by our diversity and how well we interact across racial and national lines. I tell them that our diversity comes from our focus on Jesus. "For God so loved the world,"[187] John tells us. When we focus on our praise, worship, and obedience to Jesus, we will take on his heart for the world and become more diverse.

When diversity and inclusion become our goals, then holiness and righteousness become secondary. The desire for diversity and inclusion leads to toleration of false religions and immoral lifestyles. This is what happens when we worship false idols. Diversity in the church is not the goal but it is a byproduct of the goal to draw near to Jesus.

In an international church, we build relationships across national and racial lines that go very deep because we are bonded at the heart level by our mutual love for Jesus. This gives us an experience of unity in the midst of our diversity.

TRANSLATION

Andrew Walls has written about the incarnation being the first translation of the gospel. I mentioned this in the section on community, but I want to

---

[186] The General Assembly Committee on Representation (GACOR) advises, consults with, and guides the General Assembly of the Presbyterian Church (U.S.A.) and its constituent parts on matters of inclusion, participation, and representation at all levels of church leadership and decision making. Its mission supports the mandate of the Book of Order (G-3.0103); "Committee on Representation," *PCUSA Office of the General Assembly*, http://oga.pcusa.org/section/committees/committee-representation/.

[187] John 3:16.

come back to it again. "Christian faith rests on a divine act of translation: 'the Word became flesh, and dwelt among us.'" [188] Any confidence we have in the translatability of the Bible rests on that prior act of translation. There is a history of translation of the Bible because there was a translation of the Word into flesh." [189]

The translation of the gospel is not merely a helpful tool, it is indispensable. Andrew Walls points out that "Christian faith must go on being translated, must continuously enter into vernacular culture and interact with it, or it withers and fades." [190]

This is seen in the earliest sites of Christian faith. What is the state of the church in Jerusalem, Bethlehem, Nazareth? We go to Turkey to visit the sites of the churches of Revelation and the ruins of Ephesus where Paul preached for three years. These areas of the world are now listed as among the least reached regions of the world. This can be viewed as a defeat for Christian faith but Andrew Walls makes the observation that this reflects the nature of Christian faith:

> Islam can point to a steady geographical progression from its birthplace and from its earliest years. And over all these years it has hitherto not had many territorial losses to record. Whereas the Jerusalem of the apostles has fallen, the Mecca of the prophet remains inviolate. When it comes to sustaining congregations of the faithful, Christianity does not appear to possess the same resilience as Islam. It decays and withers in its very heartlands, in the areas where it appears to have had the profoundest cultural effects. Crossing cultural boundaries, it then takes root anew on the margins of those areas, and beyond. Islamic expansion is progressive; Christian expansion is serial . . . the New Testament is clear that God can dispense even with self-important Christian communities, and that God depends on no single instrument. [191]

Christian faith is not dependent on institutions; it is dependent on a relationship. Corrie ten Boom wrote that "God has no grandchildren." [192]

---

[188] John 1:14.

[189] Walls, *Missionary Movement*, 26.

[190] Andrew Walls, *The Cross-Cultural Process in Christian History* (Maryknoll, NY: Orbis, 2002), 29.

[191] Walls, *Cross-Cultural Process*, 13.

[192] Corrie ten Boom, *Each New Day* (Grand Rapids, MI: Revell, 1977), 137.

Whereas Islam has children and grandchildren, Christian faith does not. This means that each generation and each culture must hear the gospel and respond. Christian faith cannot be franchised because there is no one Christian culture. Walls writes that,

> Each phase of Christian history has seen a transformation of Christianity as it has entered and penetrated another culture. There is no such thing as "Christian culture" or "Christian civilization" in the sense that there is an Islamic culture, and an Islamic civilization. There have been several different Christian civilizations already; there may yet be many more. The reason for this lies in the infinite translatability of the Christian faith. Islam, the only other faith hitherto to make a comparable impact in such global terms, can produce a single recognizable culture (recognizable despite local assimilations and variations) across its huge geographical spread. This has surely something to do with the ultimate untranslatablity of its charter document, the Qur'an. The Christian Scriptures, by contrast, are open to translation; nay, the great Act of which Christian faith rests, the Word becoming flesh and pitching tent among us, is itself an act of translation.[193]

In a homogenous church, the necessary translation of the gospel is not so clear. The status quo has an easier time ruling and the motto of the church can be what has been called the seven last words of the church, "We have always done it that way." In an international church "the way we have always done it" is challenged by all the threads of Christian expression and culture that interact. We are challenged and adapt. We are exposed to all the translations of the gospel into cultures and have to ask ourselves what is at the core of what we believe.

This leads to the richness of life in an international church. Walls comments, "It is a delightful paradox that the more Christ is translated into the various thought forms and life systems which form our various national identities, the richer all of us will be in our common Christian identity. The Word became flesh, and dwelt among us—and we beheld *his* glory, full of grace and truth."[194]

CORE OF FAITH

The work of the Holy Spirit is to unite us, but what we see in the church is separation and disunity. The lack of unity in the church and the bitter

---

193   Walls, *Missionary Movement*, 22–23.
194   Walls, *Missionary Movement*, 54.

theological fights between churches has disturbed church leaders for a long time. This is poked fun at in what the comedian Emo Phillips calls the "best God joke ever."

A man is walking across a bridge, when he sees another guy about to jump off.

"Hey, man" he says, "you don't have to do that."

"Why not?" the other guy says, "I've got nothing to live for. I lost my job, I'm bankrupt, my wife left me and took the kids, my car threw a rod, and my dog just died. My life totally sucks."

"But God still loves you," the man says, "you believe in God, don't you?"

"Well, I guess so," the guy says.

"Tell me, are you a Christian?"

"Yes" the guy answers.

"Well, so am I!" the man says. "Catholic or Protestant?"

"I'm Protestant"

"Well, so am I!" "Methodist, or Baptist, or Presbyterian?"

"I'm Baptist."

"Well, so am I!" "Northern or Southern Baptist?"

"Northern Baptist."

"Well so am I!" "Northern fundamentalist, liberal, or reformed?"

"Northern fundamentalist."

"Well, so am I!" "Northern fundamentalist eastern region, or Great Lakes region?"

"Northern fundamentalist, eastern region."

"Well, so am I!" "Northern fundamentalist, eastern region conference of 1898, or conference of 1912?"

"Northern fundamentalist, eastern region, conference of 1912." "Die, heretic!" the man says, and pushes him off the bridge.[195]

In *Spiritual Dynamics*, Richard Lovelace writes about the concern of the Puritan leaders, Richard Baxter and Cotton Mather, for church unity:

[Baxter] labored for years to devise a basis for a comprehensive national church which would avoid sectarian division and yet permit a wide diversity of practice anchored to a base of radical orthodoxy. A

---

[195] Emo Phillips, "The Best God Joke Ever—And It's Mine!" *The Guardian*, posted September 29, 2005, http://www.theguardian.com/stage/2005/sep/29/comedy.religion.

great deal of his energy was spent in seeking a core of doctrine around which all English Christians could unite, according to the formula of Rupert Meldenius: "Unity in essentials, liberty in incidentals, and in all things charity."

Baxter's concerns were picked up in America by Cotton Mather, whose vision of a revived church at the close of history involved the spiritual unification of Protestantism around the minimal core of doctrine essential to securing vital Christian piety. Mather compared the state of sectarian division with the church to warring tribes of bees, fighting one another because of differences in scent among the various hives. Just as the bees might be calmed and pacified by the sprinkling of a perfume which would make friend and enemy smell the same, Mather reasoned that an outpouring of the Holy Spirit which would create genuine godliness among Christians of differing minor persuasions might enable all of these to detect Christ in one another and attain unity.[196]

In a search for unity, Baxter and Mather sought a core doctrine around which the church could unite. This is the point Jeremiah Burroughs made. Because the Bible is not clear on some issues it is inevitable that there will be disagreement on secondary matters, but these disagreements should not disrupt Christian unity. There is not disagreement that Christians need a core around which they can unite, the devil is in the details (idiom intended).

Paul wrote to Timothy, "Watch your life and doctrine closely. Persevere in them, because if you do, you will save both yourself and your hearers."[197] Paul was clearly concerned about correct doctrine. He wrote his letter to the Galatians in defense of salvation by faith and strongly condemned (*anathema esto*) those who were attempting to inflict Jewish law on Gentile believers.

While doctrine is important, so is unity. How then do the two function together? When there is a doctrinal dispute, should the cause of unity override the theological divide? If unity prevails and the theology of the church stretches to include every doctrine, what happens to the purity of the church? These are serious questions and in an international church we are brought face-to-face with them.

---

[196] Richard Lovelace, *Dynamics of Spiritual Life: An Evangelical Theology of Renewal* (Downers Grove, IL: IVP, 1979), 296.
[197] 1 Timothy 4:16.

What is the function of doctrine? Is it to be right and correct? I don't think so. Doctrine is useful only as it leads us to Christ and into greater intimacy with him. Doctrine does not have a life of its own. Doctrine is a tool to help us draw closer to God. It is not an idol to be worshiped.

This leads then to considering what doctrines are useful in leading us to Christ and greater intimacy with him and what doctrines are interesting, speculative, but not critical. What is the core and what lies outside the core? Richard Lovelace writes:

> Another matter which must be given careful consideration is the very problematic issue of defining the breadth of the circle of permissible doctrinal and behavioral variation within the church, which determines the point at which discipline must be brought to bear. Most of us are ready to accept Calvin's advice and put up with "tolerable stupidities"; our only question is the size and content of this category.[198]

I find it helpful to talk about core issues versus denominational distinctives. Core doctrine is the absolute essential doctrine that draws me to Christ and encourages me to live my life for him. Core doctrines bring unity in the world-wide church. Denominational distinctives are doctrines that separate us from each other. How can we distinguish between these two? One general guideline is that core issues are where Evangelicals and Pentecostals are in agreement. When they disagree about a theological issue it is identified as peripheral.

The Apostles' Creed is a good summary of the historical core of Christian faith around which the church can unite:

> I believe in God, the Father Almighty, Maker of heaven and earth,
> And in Jesus Christ, His only son, our Lord,
> Who was conceived by the Holy Spirit,
> Born of the Virgin Mary, suffered under Pontius Pilate,
> Was crucified, dead, and buried; he descended into hell;
> The third day He rose again from the dead;
> He ascended into heaven, and sits on the right hand of God the Father Almighty,
> From there He shall come to judge the living and the dead.
> I believe in the Holy Spirit, the Holy Universal Church,
> The communion of saints, the forgiveness of sins,
> The resurrection of the body, and the life everlasting.
> Amen.

---

[198] Lovelace, *Dynamics of Spiritual Life*, 331.

If the majority of our preaching focuses on this core, then we will build life into the church. But if a large part of our preaching focuses on what makes us different from other Christian denominations, than we are breeding disunity.

The Holy Spirit puts in us a desire for unity but our human natures fight for what we are so sure is the "truth." When I was an MDiv student at Gordon-Conwell, I took church history from Richard Lovelace. Perhaps the most important lesson I learned came one day when he was talking about Luther, Calvin, Augustine, Cyprian, Tertullian, and other church leaders. He pointed out the particular part of theology that was faulty for each of these men, and I remember sitting there thinking that each of these men was far more intelligent than I am. Who was I to think that I could be the first person in church history to have everything sorted out properly? I am convinced that some of what I believe is wrong. This is true for every person alive. None of us has a perfect grasp of truth. This may be true for some aspect of what I consider to be core theology, but it is certainly true for some aspects of what I view as peripheral theology. This tells me we have to hold our peripheral theology with a measure of humility.

When the PCUSA sets up a commission to discover if Christ is the only way to salvation, the core is being violated. The prevalent belief in universalism in the PCUSA is a violation of the core.[199] When a church questions whether Jesus is the divine Son of God, the core is being violated. Lovelace writes, "On issues such as unbelief in the deity of Christ and his bodily resurrection, however, it seems fairly evident that Evangelicals would have to take a clear disciplinary stance or risk violation of the gospel."[200]

What are not core issues? The baptism of the Holy Spirit is not a core issue. Right away, anyone from a Pentecostal background will disagree. This is certainly a core issue for Pentecostals. But I say again that when Pentecostals and Evangelicals do not agree on an issue, it is not a core issue. What happens in communion is not a core issue. Baptism by immersion or sprinkling, as an adult or as an infant, is not a core issue. Women preaching in the church is not a core issue. Some believe God created the universe six or seven thousand years ago in six twenty-four hour days and others believe the world is 14 billion years

---

[199] This was my observation in the Upper Ohio Valley Presbytery (1980–1985) as candidates for ordination were questioned on the floor of Presbytery. The 112th General Assembly (1972) asked the Permanent Theological Committee to write a report on the doctrine of universalism and while the conclusion was to say that salvation was a mystery, the fact that it was asked to write this report indicates it was a wide-spread theology of the church that had not diminished ten years later.

[200] Lovelace, *Dynamics of Spiritual Life*, 331.

old and life on earth developed through a process of evolution. God created. This is a core belief. But how he created is not a core issue. A particular millennial position is not a core issue.

In all these issues, parts of the church will insist that their particular theological issue is a core issue and will quote Scripture to support their position. People are happy to say there is a core, as long as their particular doctrine is included in the core. But once again, I go back to the fact that followers of Jesus do not interpret the Bible verses quoted in support of these theological issues in the same way. (This is one of Burrough's principles, that some divisions among Christians are due to human weakness and sin, but there are some matters on which the Bible is simply not clear.) This tells me that these issues are peripheral, not core issues.

Core issues do make a difference. It is a matter of eternal life and death if I deny the deity of Jesus and the work of the Holy Spirit. This is clearly worth fighting for. But what is the harm done if we are wrong about any of these peripheral issues? What difference does it make how I am baptized? Are those who were sprinkled as infants and then confirmed as adults less committed to Christ than those who were baptized at the age of ten or eleven? Are those who have not experienced the baptism of the Holy Spirit less Spirit-filled than those who have? If a woman preaches, will God not speak through her? It is not apparent that belief in any of these peripheral doctrinal issues makes a substantive difference in the work of Jesus to build his kingdom.

So why fight to the death over peripheral issues? Why separate from each other over these issues? Why divide the body of Christ over nonessential issues? When I read the pages of *Christianity Today* and see who has been denied a position because of one of these issues, I grieve for the church.[201] And I believe God grieves as well. We were created to be in unity as the Triune God exists in unity and when we separate from each other over nonessential issues, we have unnecessarily broken the unity of Christ's body, the Church.

Lovelace generously suggests that those who hold too strictly to secondary matters "had better follow their bent and peacefully secede to some smaller denomination attempting to give a pure witness to this tradition."[202]

One of the strengths of an international church, especially one that has a great diversity because there are no other options, is that we gradually

---

[201] One example of this is the dismissal of a professor at Cedarville University because of a paper he wrote questioning a historical Adam and Eve. Melissa Steffan, "Crisis of Faith Statements," Christianity Today, posted November 2012, http://www.christianitytoday.com/ct/2012/november/crisis-of-faith-statements.html.

[202] Lovelace, *Dynamics of Spiritual Life*, 331.

pick away the peripheral doctrines until we are left with the beautiful core. This is not in any way a reduction of what we believe. As we each push to the side our peripheral doctrine, each of us illuminates the part of the core our denominational perspective has magnified. As a consequence, together we help each other to see a more complete, greater core than we had seen before.

Richard Lovelace writes,

> There are really two different and equally reasonable approaches to forming a denominational structure. One is to define as fully as possible the system of truth in Scripture and gather a group of Christians around this as a voluntary association of witnesses to one strain of Christianity. The other is to seek out the minimal circle of biblical truth which guarantees the honor of God and the spiritual health of believers, and to make this a rallying point for the largest possible number of Christians, seeking to make the visible church approximate the invisible as closely as possible.[203]

If the decision is to focus on one strain of Christianity, then it is wise to follow the guidelines of Jeremiah Burroughs and keep unity with other strains. In international churches, we take the second approach which allows us to experience more fully the relationships we will have in heaven.

One of the advantages of this second approach is that international churches help us to be more Christian and less denominational. I have observed that those from denominational backgrounds living in Morocco tend to be less dogmatic than their counterparts in their home country. I think this is because when we are in our denominational church, our denominational distinctives are continually being reinforced. But in an international church those distinctives are continually being challenged. There are people who have not been "baptized in the Holy Spirit" and do not speak in tongues, but it is clear that they are Spirit-filled and are being Spirit-led. There are women who preach effectively and God's truth comes through them.

It is painfully ironic that the Holy Spirit who was sent to unite us, to make us one body, has become a source of bitter division. Jesus said to remember him when we eat the bread and drink from the cup.[204] And yet some parts of the Christian Church do not permit those outside of their particular branch of

---

[203] Lovelace, *Dynamics of Spiritual Life*, 312.
[204] Luke 22:19.

the church to share in this meal. I want to focus my energy and gifts on doctrine that brings unity and life to the church of Jesus.

DISENCULTURATION

The process of focusing on the core of our faith involves stripping away the cultural additions to the gospel, what Richard Lovelace calls disenculturation, one of the secondary elements of renewal.[205] The international church is, once again, a great environment for this to happen.

Lovelace talks about the process by which the gospel becomes destructively enculturated by the culture to which it has come. Like barnacles that attach themselves to the wooden hull of a sailing vessel, cultural values attach themselves to the gospel. If the values are good or benign, they decorate the gospel and make it unique. But if they are ungodly values, they weaken the gospel and make it less effective in the spiritual transformation of lives. If the ship, to use Lovelace's analogy, is to sail fast, the barnacles must be removed and that is the process of disenculturation.

The difficulty comes in trying to understand what part of our gospel is enculturated. Lesslie Newbigin writes that "trying to criticize one's own culture is like trying to push a bus while you're sitting in it."[206] There is a proverb, attributed to the Chinese, that says, "If you want to know what water is, don't ask the fish."

David Foster Wallace, an American writer, illustrated this in a speech he gave: "There are these two young fish swimming along, and they happen to meet an older fish swimming the other way, who nods at them and says, 'Morning, boys, how's the water?' And the two young fish swim on for a bit, and then eventually one of them looks over at the other and goes, 'What the hell is water?'"[207] Fish know very little about water because they are never not in water. Land creatures know more about water. We know it is wet. We know that it reflects light. We know that it refreshes. We know you cannot hold it without it slipping through your fingers. Fish do not know these things.

The same is true for us in our culture. It is difficult to analyze our own cultural values. We may be able to look at popular entertainment in the U.S. and see that individualism is a value with Clint Eastwood as our cultural idol. He doesn't need anyone, and he can take care of things by himself. Is this a

[205]   Richard Lovelace, *Dynamics of Spiritual Life*, 184–200.
[206]   Lesslie Newbigin, *Gospel in a Pluralist Society*, 95.
[207]   David Foster Wallace, "Plain Old Untrendy Troubles and Emotions," *The Guardian*, http://www.guardian.co.uk/books/2008/sep/20/fiction.

Christian value? Not at all. God created us in community and he created us to be dependent on one another. Asians and Africans see this aspect of Western culture much more clearly than Westerners. On the other hand, Westerners see very clearly the materialistic effect of the health and wealth gospel in Nigeria and other African countries. Newbigin adds, "In Indian society… missionaries have attacked such deeply entrenched elements of public life as caste, dowry, child marriage, and the immolation of widows. In Africa they have similarly thrown their weight against polygamy and the slave trade."[208]

But in the homogenous churches of the world, where do we get the opportunity to do this? When do we have the opportunity to sit with each other and share our stories and learn from each other? Missionaries have had this privilege. Lesslie Newbigin describes this benefit of cross-cultural experience:

> What can also happen is that the missionary, and through him the church he represents, can become aware of the element of syncretism in his own Christianity, of the extent to which his culture had been allowed to determine the nature of the gospel he preaches, instead of being brought under judgment by that gospel. If this happens, great possibilities for mutual correction open up. Each side, perceiving Christ through the spectacle of one culture, can help the other to see how much the vision has been blurred or distorted. This kind of mutual correction is at the very heart of the ecumenical movement when it is true to itself.[209]

When I discussed this with Richard Lovelace in 1985, I thought it would be wonderful to sit down with followers of Jesus from many different cultures, nations, and denominations so we could discuss and find out the cultural attachments to our gospel. The result would be to arrive at a more pure gospel. That privilege has been mine these last fifteen years.

PILGRIMAGE
Pilgrimages in the early centuries of the church were made to visit sites associated with Jesus. Some people made long pilgrimages from Europe to Jerusalem. In the Middle Ages, it became very popular for pilgrims to set out from France and walk the 1,600 kilometers (1,000 miles) to Santiago de Compostela, located in the northwest of Spain. This pilgrimage took about

[208] Leslie Newbigin, *Foolishness to the Greeks: The Gospel and Western Culture* (Grand Rapids, MI: Eerdmans, 1986), 95.

[209] Newbigin, 9.

two and a half months to complete and along the way pilgrims could visit the cathedrals that contained what were said to be relics of Jesus and his disciples. Some set out on a second pilgrimage, from Santiago de Compostela to Rome, and then a third, from Rome to Jerusalem.

Pilgrimage continues to be popular in the modern world. A Baptist couple from the northwest of the U.S. wrote an account of their more than 4,000 mile pilgrimage in 1986–1987 when they walked from Paris to Santiago de Compostela to Rome to Jerusalem in one year.[210] Those who live overseas can relate to this because they have left the comfort of their home and set out on a journey.

For followers of Jesus, pilgrimage begins when we realize the world is not as it should be and we call out for help. Psalms 120–134 are the Psalms of Ascent, sung by Jesus and other Jewish pilgrims who ascended to Jerusalem for the three annual festivals. The first verses of the first psalm of ascent are a cry for help, "I call on the LORD in my distress, and he answers me. Save me, O LORD, from lying lips and from deceitful tongues."[211] We are distressed with the way the world operates and we want something better.

This is where pilgrimage begins. This is where all followers of Jesus start. God has put eternity in our hearts and we know, deep inside of us, that this is not how we are meant to live. We are not content to sit any longer in the mess of this world and so we set our sights on something better. We turn from the pursuit of our own self-interests and set our focus on a new destination, heading for a world where there are no lying lips and deceitful tongues. We are still engaged in the world but it no longer holds ultimate importance for us.

Saul of Tarsus set out for Damascus to return Jewish followers of the Way to their senses, to help them, once again, set their hearts on pilgrimage to the Temple in Jerusalem. But as Tom Wright writes in his book on pilgrimage,

> It was Saul himself, not the Damascus Christians, who became the surprised and reluctant pilgrim. As he journeyed away from the Land, away from the Holy city, away from the Temple, he was confronted by the living God: as he would later write, in a passage full of echoes of that first sight of the risen Jesus, he was faced with "the light of the knowledge of the glory of God in the face of Jesus the Messiah" (2 Corinthians 4.6). People went on pilgrimage in order to come face to

---

[210]   Karen Whitehill, *A Walk Across Holy Ground* (Wheaton, IL: Tyndale), 1990.
[211]   Psalm 120:1-2.

face with the living God; Saul realized the pilgrim's goal while going, literally and metaphorically, in the opposite direction.[212]

Wright points out that Saul not only began a pilgrimage with his conversion, but with his turning around, his direction changed. No longer was Jerusalem the destination. "It is the heavenly Jerusalem, he wrote to the Galatians, that is the mother of us all: the coming city of God, the city that already exists in the purposes of God and will one day be revealed, with ourselves as its citizens."[213]

Like Paul, each follower of Jesus sets out on a journey to God, following the path of Jesus who said, "I am the way and the truth and the life. No one comes to the Father except through me."[214] We are pilgrims on a pilgrimage and our central identity is that we are daughters and sons of God. More than any of the other roles we play, this defines who we are and who we are to be. Before I am a husband, a father, a father-in-law, a grandfather, a friend, a pastor, before any of these, I am a son of God. That is who I am.

To have our central identity be that we are daughters and sons of God means our central occupation is being on pilgrimage. We are moving from where we are now to where we will live for eternity. We are heading home to be with our father. This is our chief occupation, more important than any job or any career we have.

Being on pilgrimage helps us to understand how to relate to those whose pilgrimage is not following Jesus to the Celestial City. As pilgrims, we are, as D. T. Niles famously said, "one beggar telling another beggar where he found bread."[215] This perspective transforms how we relate to all pilgrims. Followers of Jesus, Muslims, Hindus, and others face the same problem: we are separated from God, however God is understood to be. Muslims submit to Allah and the Five Pillars of Islam. Buddhists follow the Eightfold Path with the goal of escaping the endless cycle of reincarnation. Hindus generate karma so they can be born into the Brahmin class and enter into Nirvana. Followers of Jesus understand that we are incapable, on our own, of bridging the distance between ourselves and God. We accept with gratitude the grace of God that allows us to draw near to him through the work Jesus has done to save us from eternal separation from God.

---

[212] Tom Wright, *The Way of the Lord* (London, UK: Triangle, 1999), 15.

[213] Wright, 16.

[214] John 14:6.

[215] D. T. Niles, *That They May Have Life* (New York: Harper, 1951), 96.

When we meet pilgrims of other faiths, it is helpful to share with each other how we understand that we can draw near to God and how we think we will arrive to the Celestial City, reach paradise, or become one with the consciousness of God. This creates an open discussion in which our deep human needs are addressed and our common identity as pilgrims is acknowledged.

Understanding that we are on pilgrimage helps us to realize that religion is a search for truth, not a competition for truth. If we treat religion as a competition for truth, then we fight for converts. We are encouraged when a Muslim becomes a follower of Jesus, and we are discouraged when a Christian becomes a Muslim. The way we act seems to indicate that we think truth is arrived at democratically; whoever gets the most votes is most true. But truth is not determined democratically; What is true is true, no matter how many people believe it to be true. The goal, at the end of my life, is not to have Christianity win. The goal is for me to be with God. How will this happen?

The interactions that come with being part of an international church bring us into relationships that stretch us and challenge us to think about who we are and where we are heading. Because we are distanced from the culture of our faith we grew up with and because we are not at home in the culture in which we live, it becomes more clear that we are pilgrims, heading toward the Celestial City.

ALIENS

When we set out on pilgrimage, we come to the understanding that we are aliens in this world. As pilgrims, we turn from our focus on the world and all it has to offer and turn our sights toward our heavenly destination. We come to realize that, in the words of Randy Alcorn, "[We] are made for a person and a place. Jesus is the person. Heaven is the place."[216] We are no longer at home in the world. "Friends, this world is not your home, so don't make yourselves cozy in it."[217] "This 'insider world' is not our home. We have our eyes peeled for the City about to come."[218]

While we remain citizens of earth, we take on a dual citizenship in heaven. We remain with earthly responsibilities but we realize that our jobs and our careers do not have ultimate importance. We are passing through. We are grateful for the temporal, material blessings of God in this life and enjoy the pleasure and meaning they bring to us. We realize, however, that they will not last. They will be left behind when we make our final transition to the eternal

---

[216] Randy Alcorn, *Heaven* (Wheaton, IL: Tyndale, 2004), 37.

[217] 1 Peter 2:11 (The Message).

[218] Hebrews 13:14 (The Message).

kingdom. In this we model ourselves after the heroes of the faith listed in Hebrews 11:

> All these people were still living by faith when they died. They did not receive the things promised; they only saw them and welcomed them from a distance. And they admitted that they were aliens and strangers on earth. People who say such things show that they are looking for a country of their own. If they had been thinking of the country they had left, they would have had opportunity to return. Instead, they were longing for a better country—a heavenly one. Therefore God is not ashamed to be called their God, for he has prepared a city for them.[219]

In Psalm 120, the first of the Psalms of Ascent sung by pilgrims on their way up to Jerusalem for the three annual festivals, the psalmist mentions two alternatives to setting out on pilgrimage that are destructive to us.[220] The first of these is accommodation. "Too long have I lived among those who hate peace."[221] Andrew Walls writes,

> Throughout Christian history two forces are distinguishable in constant tension. One is an indigenizing principle, a homing instinct, which creates in diverse communities a sense that the Church belongs there, that it is "ours." The other is a "pilgrim" principle that creates within the Christian community the sense that it is not fully at home in this world, so that it comes into tension with its society from its loyalty to Christ.[222]

We know that we are aliens, that we do not belong to this world, and so we do not settle down and adapt to the culture. We are pilgrims and pilgrims move forward as they hold on to the values of their destination. Pilgrims are heading toward the kingdom of God and do their best to live by those values while they are on pilgrimage through this life on earth.

One of the best examples of this in the Bible is Lot, the nephew of Abraham. Abraham was a pilgrim. When God called him, he left his birthplace and

---

[219] Hebrews 11:13–16.

[220] Derek Kidner, *Psalms 73–150: A Commentary On Books III–V of the Psalms* (Downers Grove, IL: IVP, 1975), 430.

[221] Psalm 120:6.

[222] Walls, *Missionary Movement*, 53–54.

traveled to Canaan. As Abraham traveled, he build altars where he worshiped God. When you read through the account of Abraham in Genesis, over and over again, Abraham built altars. In Genesis 12:7 Abraham built an altar. In Genesis 12:8 he built an altar. In Genesis 13:4 and 18 he built altars. This stands in remarkable contrast to the life of Lot.

When Abraham and Lot became too wealthy and the herdsmen of Lot were fighting with the herdsmen of Abraham, Abraham called Lot to a mountain overlooking the valley of Jordan and asked him to choose what land he would take. Lot chose the lush, fertile land of the valley in which lay the cities of Sodom and Gomorrah that were later destroyed because, as it is written in Genesis 13, "Now the men of Sodom were wicked and were sinning greatly against the Lord."[223]

After Lot chose the plains of the Jordan valley, we read that "Lot lived among the cities of the plain and pitched his tents near Sodom."[224] Lot made his choice and then Abraham built an altar and worshiped the Lord, but Lot pitched his tents near Sodom.

Later there was a battle and Lot and his possessions were captured. "They also carried off Abram's nephew Lot and his possessions, since he was living in Sodom."[225] Lot pitched his tents near Sodom and when the kings captured him he had moved and was now living in Sodom.

When angels arrived to destroy Sodom and Gomorrah because of the great evil in those cities, where was Lot to be found? "The two angels arrived at Sodom in the evening, and Lot was sitting in the gateway of the city."[226] Lot pitched his tent near Sodom, then lived in Sodom, and finally sat as a city elder in the gates of Sodom. Lot walked by Sodom, then stood in Sodom, and finally sat in Sodom.[227] Lot never set out on pilgrimage. Unlike the writer of Psalm 120, he did not get tired of living among those who hated peace. Pilgrims do not settle down and accommodate to the culture, they move forward, bringing the values of the kingdom of God into their world. Pilgrims are aliens and strangers, moving through the land, not accommodating to the culture. Peter encouraged us to take this view of ourselves in his letter: "Dear friends, I urge you, as aliens

---

[223] Genesis 13:13.

[224] Genesis 13:12.

[225] Genesis 14:12.

[226] Genesis 19:1.

[227] "Blessed is the man who does not walk in the counsel of the wicked or stand in the way of sinners or sit in the seat of mockers," Psalm 1:1.

and strangers in the world, to abstain from sinful desires, which war against your soul."[228]

Those who are part of international church communities have uprooted themselves from comfortable routines. As aliens in a foreign land, they are stripped of accommodating behaviors. They celebrate different holidays, eat different foods, shop in different stores or markets. All of this reminds them that they do not fit in. They do not belong. It comes as a shock to the system in what is called "culture shock." This disruption helps followers of Jesus to consider who they are, who they belong to, and where they are heading.

LIVING IN THE PRESENT

Jesus taught that "no one pours new wine into old wineskins. If he does, the new wine will burst the skins, the wine will run out and the wineskins will be ruined. No, new wine must be poured into new wineskins. And no one after drinking old wine wants the new, for he says, 'The old is better.'"[229] International churches have a very limited history, and with the high rate of turnover, international churches have less old wineskins to deal with. They tend to live in the present. This is one of the advantages of international churches.

David Olson in *The American Church in Crisis* pointed out that the growth rate in churches is highest in the early years of a church's existence. "Once churches reach 40 years of age, on average they enter a period of long and sustained decline."[230] The first year averages 12 percent growth and then goes to 9 percent in years two and three, and then 4–6 percent in years four to ten. Years 11–30 have a 1 percent growth rate and years 31–40 have almost a 0 percent growth rate. From that point on, in years 41–400, the average church drops in membership about 1 percent a year.

Why is this? Has the culture rejected the gospel or has the church failed to effectively communicate the gospel to a new generation? Or has the community changed and a new culture has moved in, and the church has not been willing to adapt?

It seems to me that in each generation God seeks to rescue that generation and build his church. And he desires to use his children to work with him in building his church. But God has no loyalty to man-made institutions. We see things from a temporal point of view and have an exaggerated sense of

---

[228] 1 Peter 2:11.

[229] Luke 5:37–39.

[230] David T. Olson, *The American Church in Crisis: Groundbreaking Research Based On a National Database of Over 200,000 Churches* (Grand Rapids, MI: Zondervan, 2008), 83.

the importance of institutions we have built, but God has a very different perspective.

When a gardener steps into his toolshed to see what tools are available to begin working in his garden that spring, what does he do if he finds a broken hoe? Does he begin to grieve? No. He gets a new handle or buys a new hoe. His goal is to break the ground and cultivate the soil so it will produce new fruit.

In the same way, God sets out to work in the new generation to rescue people who are lost and he uses the tools available to him. If a church is so inward focused that it cannot see the mission to reach out and save the lost, it is pushed to the side. If a Christian institution has moved from its initial mission to work with God in his rescue of people who are lost to a focus on feeding itself, it is discarded much as a broken hoe.

What happens to churches and church institutions that move from an initial focus on God's mission to an inability to work with God on his mission? Olson writes, "Like aging athletes, many churches over 40 are less flexible, move more slowly, and no longer respond well to change."[231] And, in fact, "The older the members of a church are, the slower the church grows."[232]

Religious experience is inevitably institutionalized and the institutionalization of religious experience leads to spiritual deadness. When we begin our Christian life reading a certain translation of the Bible, we stick with that to the end of our life and disdain new translations of the Bible. When we grow up singing hymns, we resist the new praise choruses.

My wife's grandfather grew up in the Lutheran Church and told us once that when he was a young man he had been a leader in the church to bring in the new Lutheran liturgy. Now in his 80s there was another new Lutheran liturgy and he was among those opposed to the new liturgy. This is the pattern we follow. In our youth we look for what is new and communicates to us; in our older years we cling to what we have known.

What would it be like if our lifespan were doubled? What would happen if we lived to be 160–200 rather than our 80–100 years we now live? If our lifespans were doubled, it is likely the church would be much further behind in its impact on the world because we would continue to resist adapting to the culture for a much longer time. Fortunately for the church, we begin to die off in our sixties and the church is spared a dominating percentage of the church that argues that what was good enough for us is good enough for the new generation.

---

[231] Olson, *American Church in Crisis*, 84.
[232] Olson, 85.

Many years ago when I was reading through Leviticus and came to the year of Jubilee in Leviticus 25, I thought that it would be good if this was applied to all Christian institutions. If every fifty years the church and all parachurch organizations had to start all over, we would be much better off.

This is the advantage of most international churches. We do not have endowment funds that perpetuate our existence long after we have ceased to be an effective tool in the work of Jesus. We do not have a long history on which we stand. As I have mentioned, with the high rate of transition in most international churches, both members and pastors, it is difficult to go back more than a decade or two. The past for RIC is just the last couple years. Less than a quarter of those who currently attend RIC were here in 2010 when 150 foreign Christians were deported from Morocco and we were forced to leave the building where we had met for the prior thirty years. We moved to our present facility in May 2013 and that will be old history by the summer of 2015.

The advantage of this is that we are more open to the change new members bring with them. Once again, our circumstances force us to live a healthier church life.

Those who attend international churches are, for the most part, people who will be in that church for just a few short years. The past has faded and they will not be there in the future so they live in the present. As they interact with the indigenous population, they realize that they do not belong to that culture. They are aliens and this helps them to identify with those in the Bible who set out on pilgrimage to a land that is promised but not yet at hand. As they interact with fellow pilgrims who have come from many different cultures, they are challenged about what it is they believe and come to a more clear vision of the core of Christian faith around which followers of Jesus in the world can unite. They are delighted by the different expressions of culture with which the gospel has been decorated and encouraged by a common identity as followers of Jesus. The community that develops as relationships are built across national, denominational, and racial lines makes our praise and worship of the eternal, Triune God, Father, Son, and Holy Spirit, a rich, deep experience.

Being part of an international church helps us see our faith with very different eyes. And it helps us to move closer to the community life I believe God intends for us to live. Once again, this is not to our credit. The dynamics of international churches are thrust upon us. We are the grateful recipients of the blessing that comes from living in a community that reflects the rich diversity of God's creation.

ACKNOWLEDGMENTS

I want to thank Rabat International Church for allowing me to take the time to work on my DMin and to write this guide that was part of my thesis project. In particular, Sue Beaman, Connie Huffer, Elliot Lamptey, and Patrick Havens were of great help.

I very much appreciate the international church pastors and leaders who read and commented on *A Guide to International Church Ministry*: Greg Anderson, John Carlock, Ray Cobb, John Findley, Daphne Fisher, David Fisher, Barry Gaeddert, Wendy Haugtvedt, Roger Hesch, Deon Malan, Chris Martin, Steve McDaniel, Ken MacHarg, Steve McMichael, John Mullen, David Packer, David Pederson, Louwrens Scheepers, and an unnamed pastor exploring overseas ministry. I want to especially thank Ken MacHarg for his encouragement as a first reader of the guide.

I am deeply grateful to David Currie who was my thesis project advisor. Many times when I doubted my ability to complete my thesis project, he encouraged me and gave me direction. David is a pastor-professor and when I called to talk with him, he most often ended our conversation with prayer. He also prayed for me each week. (I think my day was Saturday.) It has been a privilege to have worked with him.

I want to thank Bruce Barton, my brother-in-law, whose company helped with the typesetting and publication of this guide. He and my sister were used by God to bring me to faith in Jesus and he has been a great friend over the years.

I also want to thank Bob Allums who encouraged me to put my thesis in book form and helped to make it accessible to interested readers. He is an encourager, like Barnabas.

Thirty-eight years ago I was fortunate enough to have married a woman who would one day be editor-in-chief of Princeton University Press—so that she would have the skills to help me with the editing of this guide. Annie's love for me and her encouragement to use my gifts allows me to do what I might not dare attempt otherwise.

BIBLIOGRAPHY

General:

Alcorn, Randy. *Heaven*. Wheaton, IL: Tyndale, 2004.

Bailey, Kenneth E. *Jesus Through Middle Eastern Eyes: Cultural Studies in the Gospels*. Downers Grove, IL: InterVarsity Press, 2008.

Bosch, David J. *A Spirituality of the Road*. Scottdale, PA: Herald Press, 1979.

Collins, Frances. *The Language of God: A Scientist Presents Evidence for Belief.* New York: Free Press, 2006.

DeYmaz, Mark, and Harry Li. *Ethnic Blends: Mixing Diversity into Your Local Church*. Grand Rapids, MI: Zondervan, 2010.

Fee, Gordon D., and Douglas Stuart. *How to Read the Bible for All Its Worth: A Guide to Understanding the Bible.* Grand Rapids, MI: Zondervan, 1982.

Fernández-Armesto, Felipe. *Near a Thousand Tables: A History of Food*. New York: Free Press, 2002.

Hauerwas, Stanley. *Christian Existence Today: Essays on Church, World and Living in Between,* Durham, NC: Labyrinth, 1988.

Hess, Melissa Brayer, and Patricia Linderman. *The Expert Expat: Your Guide to Successful Relocation Abroad*. Rev. ed. Boston, MA: Nicholas Brealey Publishing, 2007.

Hesselgrave, David J. *Communicating Christ Cross-Culturally: An Introduction to Missionary Communication*. 2nd ed. Grand Rapids, MI: Zondervan, 1991.

Huntington, Samuel P. *The Clash of Civilizations and the Remaking of World Order*. New York: Simon & Schuster, 2003.

Jenkins, Philip. *The Lost History of Christianity: The Thousand-Year Golden Age of the Church in the Middle East, Africa, and Asia—and How It Died.* New York: HarperOne, 2008.

————. *The New Faces of Christianity: Believing the Bible in the Global South.* New York: Oxford University, 2008.

Keillor, Garrison. *Lake Wobegon Days.* New York: Viking, 1985.

Keller, Timothy. *The Meaning of Marriage: Facing the Complexities of Commitment with the Wisdom of God.* New York: Dutton, 2011.

Kidner, Derek. *Psalms 73–150: A Commentary On Books III–V of the Psalms.* London, UK: InterVarsity Press, 1975.

Kohls, L. Robert. *Survival Kit for Overseas Living: For Americans Planning to Live and Work Abroad.* Yarmouth, ME: Intercultural Press, 1996.

Lovelace, Richard. *Dynamics of Spiritual Life: An Evangelical Theology of Renewal.* Downers Grove, IL: InterVarsity Press, 1979.

MacHarg, Kenneth D. *Singing the Lord's Songs in a Foreign Land: Biblical Reflections for Expatriates.* n.p.: Global Village Press. 2011.

McCullough, David. *The Greater Journey: Americans in Paris.* New York: Simon & Schuster, 2011.

Millar, Gary, and Phil Campbell. *Saving Eutychus: How to Preach God's Word and Keep People Awake.* Kingsford, Australia: Matthias Media, 2013.

Miller, Paul E. *Love Walked Among Us: Learning to Love Like Jesus.* Colorado Springs, CO: NavPress, 2001.

Mischke, Werner. *The Global Gospel: Achieving Missional Impact in Our Multicultural World.* n.p.: Mission One, 2015.

Muller, Roland. *Honor & Shame: Unlocking the Door.* n.p.: Xlibris, 2000.

————. *The Messenger, the Message, the Community: Three Critical Issues for the Cross Cultural Church-Planter.* Altona, Canada: CanBooks, 2006.

Murray, Iain H. *Revival and Revivalism: The Making and Marring of American Evangelicalism 1750–1858.* Edinburgh, Scotland: Banner of Truth, 1994.

Nathan, Rich, and Ken Wilson. *Empowered Evangelicals: Bringing Together the Best of the Evangelical and Charismatic Worlds.* Ann Arbor, MI: Vine Books, 1995.

Newbigin, Lesslie. *Foolishness to the Greeks: The Gospel and Western Culture.* Grand Rapids, MI: Eerdmans, 1986.

————. *The Gospel in a Pluralist Society.* Grand Rapids, MI: Eerdmans, 1989.

————. *The Open Secret: An Introduction to the Theology of Mission.* Rev. ed. Grand Rapids, MI: Eerdmans, 1995.

Niles, D. T. *That They May Have Life.* New York: Harper & Brothers, 1951.

Norwich, John Julius. *A Short History of Byzantium.* New York: Vintage Books, 1997.

Olson, David T. *The American Church in Crisis: Groundbreaking Research Based On a National Database of Over 200,000 Churches.* Grand Rapids, MI: Zondervan, 2008.

Ortiz, Manuel. *One New People: Models for Developing a Multiethnic Church.* Downers Grove, IL: IVP, 1996.

Packer, David. *Look Who God Let Into the Church: Understanding the Nature and Sharpening the Impact of a Multicultural Church.* n.p.: CreateSpace Independent Publishing Platform, 2013.

Packer, David., ed. *The International Pastor Experience: Testimonies from the Field.* n.p.: CreateSpace Independent Publishing Platform, 2015.

Pederson, David. *Expatriate Ministry: Inside the Church of the Outsiders.* Seoul, Korea: Korean Center for World Missions, 1999.

Pollock, David C., and Ruth E. Van Reken. *Third Culture Kids: Growing up Among Worlds.* Boston, MA: Nicholas Brealey Publishing, 2009.

Potter, Ellis. *3 Theories of Everything.* n.p.: Destineé S.A., 2012.

Reeves, Michael. *Delighting in the Trinity: An Introduction to the Christian Faith.* Downers Grove, IL: InterVarsity, 2012.

Rhodes, Stephen A. *Where the Nations Meet: The Church in a Multicultural World.* Downers Grove, IL: IVP, 1998.

Richards, E. Randolph, and Brandon J. O'Brien. *Misreading Scripture with Western Eyes: Removing Cultural Binders to Better Understand the Bible.* Downers Grove, IL: InterVarsity, 2012.

Saint-Exupéry, Antoine de. *Wind, Sand and Stars.* London, UK: The Folio Society, 1990.

Smith, James Bryan. *Rich Mullins: A Devotional Biography: an Arrow Pointing to Heaven*. Nashville, TN: Broadman, 2000.

Sweet, Leonard. *FaithQuakes*, Nashville, TN: Abingdon, 1944.

Ten Boom, Corrie. *Each New Day*. Grand Rapids, MI: Revell, 1977.

Tennent, Timothy C. *Theology in the Context of World Christianity: How the Global Church Is Influencing the Way We Think About and Discuss Theology*. Grand Rapids, MI: Zondervan, 2007.

Volf, Miroslav. *Exclusion & Embrace: A Theological Exploration of Identity, Otherness, and Reconciliation*. Nashville, TN: Abingdon, 1996.

Wagner, C. Peter. *The Book of Acts: A Commentary*. Grand Rapids, MI: Zondervan, 2001.

Walls, Andrew. *The Cross-Cultural Process in Christian History*. Maryknoll, NY: Orbis Books, 2002.

———. *The Missionary Movement in Christian History: Studies in the Transmission of Faith*. Maryknoll, NY: Orbis Books, 1996.

Walton, John H. *Genesis*. NIVAC. Grand Rapids, MI: Zondervan, 2001.

Whitehill, Karen. *A Walk Across Holy Ground*. Wheaton, IL: Tyndale, 1990.

Woo, Rodney. *The Color of Church*. Nashville, TN: Broadman, 2009.

Wright, Tom. *The Way of the Lord*. London, UK: Triangle, 1999.

Zakaria, Fareed. *The Future of Freedom: Illiberal Democracy at Home and Abroad*. New York: W. W. Norton & Company, 2004.

Specific to Islam:

Brooks, Geraldine. *Nine Parts of Desire: The Hidden World of Islamic Women*. London, UK: Penguin, 1996.

Daniel, Robin. *This Holy Seed: Faith, Hope and Love in the Early Churches of North Africa*. Harpenden, UK: Tamarisk Publications, 1993.

Doyle, Tom, and Greg Webster. *Dreams and Visions: Is Jesus Awakening the Muslim World?* Nashville, TN: Nelson, 2012.

Elass, Mateen. *Understanding the Koran: A Quick Christian Guide to the Muslim Holy Book*. Grand Rapids, MI: Zondervan, 2004.

Ende, Werner, and Udo Steinbach. *Islam in the World Today: A Handbook of Politics, Religion, Culture, and Society.* Ithaca, NY: Cornell University Press, 2010.

Garrison, David. *A Wind in the House of Islam: How God Is Drawing Muslims Around the World to Faith in Jesus Christ.* Monument, CO: WIGTake Resources, 2014.

Goldman, David. *Islam and the Bible: Why Two Faiths Collide.* Chicago: Moody, 2004.

Greear, J.D. *Breaking the Islam Code: Understanding the Soul Questions of Every Muslim.* Eugene, OR: Harvest House, 2010.

Houssney, Georges. *Engaging Islam.* Boulder, CO: Treeline Publishing, 2010.

Lewis, Bernard. *The Crisis of Islam: Holy War and Unholy Terror.* London, UK: Weidenfield & Nicolson, 2003.

———. *Cultures in Conflict: Christians, Muslims, and Jews in the Age of Discovery.* Oxford, UK: Oxford University, 1996.

———. *What Went Wrong? The Clash between Islam and Modernity in the Middle East.* Hong Kong, China: Harper Perennial, 2003.

Love, Rick. *Muslims, Magic and the Kingdom of God.* Pasadena, CA: William Carey Library, 2000.

Maalouf, Tony. *Arabs in the Shadow of Israel: The Unfolding of God's Prophetic Plan for Ishmael's Line.* Grand Rapids, MI: Kregel, 2003.

Makdisi, Ussama. *Artillery of Heaven: American Missionaries and the Failed Conversion of the Middle East.* Ithaca, NY: Cornell University, 2009.

Mallouhi, Christine A. *Waging Peace on Islam.* London, UK: Monarch Books, 2000.

Medearis, Carl. *Muslims, Christians, and Jesus: Gaining Understanding and Building Relationships.* Minneapolis, MN: Bethany House, 2008.

Menocal, María Rosa. *The Ornament of the World: How Muslims, Jews, and Christians Created a Culture of Tolerance in Medieval Spain.* New York: Little, Brown and Company, 2002.

Partner, Peter. *God of Battles: Holy Wars of Christianity and Islam.* Princeton, NJ: Princeton University, 1997.

Reston, James, Jr. *Warriors of God: Richard the Lionheart and Saladin in the Third Crusade.* New York: Anchor Books, 2001.

Satloff, Robert. *Among the Righteous: Lost Stories from the Holocaust's Long Reach into Arab Lands.* New York: PublicAffairs, 2006.

Sharkey, Heather J. *American Evangelicals in Egypt: Missionary Encounters in an Age of Empire.* Princeton, NJ: Princeton University, 2008.

Tinniswood, Adrian. *Pirates of Barbary: Corsairs, Conquests, and Captivity in the Seventeenth-Century Mediterranean.* New York: Riverhead Books, 2010.

Trousdale, Jerry. *Miraculous Movements: How Hundreds of Thousands of Muslims Are Falling in Love with Jesus.* Nashville, TN: Nelson, 2012.

Specific to Morocco:

Dann, Robert. *Pretty as a Moonlit Donkey: A Whimsical Jaunt Down the Proverbial Byways of Moroccan Folklore.* Chester, England: Jacaranda Books, 2001.

Graciet, Catherine et Éric Laurent. *Le Roi Prédateur: Main Basse sur le Maroc.* France: Seuil, 2012.

Hamilton, Richard. *The Last Storytellers: Tales from the Heart of Morocco.* London, UK: I.B. Tauris, 2013.

Hargraves, Orin. *Morocco (Culture Shock! A Survival Guide to Customs and Etiquette).* Portland, OR: Graphic Arts Center Publishing Company, 1995.

Harris, Walter. *Morocco That Was.* London, UK: Eland Books, 1921.

Howe, Marvine. *Morocco: The Islamist Awakening and Other Challenges.* Oxford: Oxford University, 2005.

King, Dean. *Skeletons on the Zahara: A True Story of Survival.* Boston, MA: Back Bay Books, 2004.

Maxwell, Gavin. *Lords of the Atlas: The Rise and Fall of the House of Glaoua 1893–1956.* London, UK: Pan Books Ltd., 1966.

Milton, Giles. *White Gold: the Extraordinary Story of Thomas Pellow and Islam's One Million White Slaves.* New York: Farrar, Straus and Giroux, 2004.

Oufkir, Malika. *Freedom: The Story of My Second Life.* New York: Miramax, 2006.

———. *Stolen Lives: Twenty Years in a Desert Jail.* New York: Miramax, 1999.

Wharton, Edith. *In Morocco.* Hopewell, NJ: Ecco Press, 1920.

CPSIA information can be obtained at www.ICGtesting.com
Printed in the USA
BVOW09s2350060216

435609BV00007B/7/P